NEW FORD BRONCO

PERFORMANCE MODIFICATIONS

Don Alexander

CarTech ®

CarTech®

CarTech®, Inc.
6118 Main Street
North Branch, MN 55056
Phone: 651-277-1200 or 800-551-4754
Fax: 651-277-1203
www.cartechbooks.com

Edit by Bob Wilson
Layout by Connie DeFlorin

ISBN 978-1-61325-843-9
Item No. SA551

Library of Congress Cataloging-in-Publication Data Available

Written, edited, and designed in the U.S.A.
Printed in China
10 9 8 7 6 5 4 3 2 1

Cover photo: Courtesy Bestop

DISTRIBUTION BY:

Europe
PGUK
63 Hatton Garden
London EC1N 8LE, England
Phone: 020 7061 1980 • Fax: 020 7242 3725
www.pguk.co.uk

Australia
Renniks Publications Ltd.
3/37-39 Green Street
Banksmeadow, NSW 2109, Australia
Phone: 2 9695 7055 • Fax: 2 9695 7355
www.renniks.com

Canada
Login Canada
300 Saulteaux Crescent
Winnipeg, MB, R3J 3T2 Canada
Phone: 800 665 1148 • Fax: 800 665 0103
www.lb.ca

CONTENTS

INTRODUCTION

In 2020, when Ford announced the production of the sixth-generation Bronco, considerable speculation erupted. How would the new Bronco compare to older versions? How would it compare to the Jeep Wrangler JL and other modern 4x4 sport utility vehicles (SUVs)? Would a V-8 engine be available? Would the front suspension be a solid axle (as is installed on the Wrangler) or independent (as is installed on most other off-road capable 4x4s)? Ford enthusiasts (and even some Jeep owners) hoped that the new Bronco would compete directly with the Jeep Wrangler.

Perhaps the most curious element of the sixth-generation Bronco announcement was the 25-year gap between the fifth-generation and sixth-generation models.

Ford also launched the Bronco Sport, which is a smaller, less-capable version of the Bronco and is based on the Ford Escape platform. The Branco is a direct competitor of the Jeep Wrangler, whereas the Bronco Sport matches more closely with the Jeep Compass or Renegade. The Bronco Sport is much smaller than the full-size Bronco, lacks a transfer case with low-range gearing, is limited to using smaller tires, and has less power. However, the Bronco Sport is capable when it is compared to the Jeep Compass, Jeep Renegade, Toyota RAV4, and other small 4x4 SUVs. (This book covers the sixth-generation full-size Bronco and not the Bronco Sport).

Ford Bronco Generations	
Generation	Year Range
First	1966-1977
Second	1978-1979
Third	1980-1986
Fourth	1987-1991
Fifth	1992-1996
Sixth	2021-present

When the sixth-generation Bronco was launched, some hardcore off-roaders were a little disappointed that the new Bronco lacked a solid front suspension system and a V-8 engine option. Admittedly, the lack of a V-8 option was a bit of disappointment—but not from a power standpoint. The sixth-generation Bronco with the twin-turbo 2.7L V-6 engine produces plenty of horsepower and torque. The issue was the sound. Old-timers love the roar of a V-8. Ford has always excelled at creating throaty, rumbling V-8 engines starting with the early Mustangs and continuing today. When a first-generation Bronco with a modified engine and exhaust fires up at a Bronco event, it attracts a large amount of attention. Conversely, when the turbos kick in on a sixth-generation Bronco, the acceleration demands attention.

The use of independent front suspension disappoints hardcore off-roaders, including me. The reduced axle articulation and more strain on the front axle's constant-velocity (CV) joints are concerning, especially when a suspension lift of more than 2 inches is installed. Ford followed the trend of every other off-road-capable modern truck and SUV by choosing independent front suspension on the Bronco.

However, the front suspension is only an issue for extreme trails that are rutted and rocky. The independent front suspension shines on the highway and when zipping across desert terrain. Handling and ride quality are significantly improved with the independent front suspension setup. Realistically, that's more important to 90 percent (or more) of the market.

At the end of the day, Ford engineers created a platform with independent front suspension to offer superior off-road capability compared to the other off-road-worthy modern trucks and SUVs. Models such as the Wildtrak and Badlands with the Sasquatch package are great right off the showroom floor. A few aftermarket upgrades for improved steering strength and underside and body protection are all that is needed to create an exceptional overlanding and off-roading rig.

Speaking of the aftermarket, the number of aftermarket companies that provide a wide range of products to improve on the already-capable Bronco challenges the range of products that is offered for other off-road vehicles, such as the Jeep Wrangler. Upgrading a sixth-generation Bronco is what this book is all about. Enjoy!

BRONCO MODELS

Ford created quite a stir when it announced the launch of the sixth-generation Bronco. Ford enthusiasts were ecstatic, Jeep owners were curious, and Stellantis (the company that owns Chrysler) was rightfully concerned.

The lineup of Bronco models has not disappointed, and the Bronco is a formidable off-road machine. However, many Jeep enthusiasts argue that the independent front suspension limits its off-road capability, which is true to a point.

Ford wisely equipped the Bronco with features that are not found on other true off-road vehicles, including Trail Turn Assist, Trail 1-Pedal Drive, and the Goes over Any Type of Terrain (G.O.A.T.) modes. These are a few examples from the forward-thinking Ford engineers, and the electronics are second to none.

The 360-degree camera with off-road views feature begs the question, "How did they do that?" Front, rear, and mirror-mounted cameras provide several views that are helpful for off-road driving. The full bird's-eye view around the vehicle from above almost defies logic (maybe they used artificial intelligence to achieve this). All in all, the Bronco fits into the off-roading world

The sixth-generation Ford Bronco offers the first real challenge to the Jeep Wrangler since the last full-size Bronco. The fifth-generation Bronco ceased production in 1996. (Photo Courtesy Ford Motor Company)

Sixth-Generation Bronco Features

According to Ford, all sixth-generation Bronco models feature some of the Ford Co-Pilot360 Technology features, which include the following:

- Pre-collision assist with automatic emergency braking
- Lane-keeping system
- Connected voice-activated, touch-screen navigation system
- SiriusXM with 360L
- Reverse parking sensors
- Trail Control (requires 10-speed transmission)

- Trail Turn Assist (requires 10-speed transmission)
- Hill Start Assist
- Post-collision braking
- Auto high-beam headlamps
- Rearview camera with backup assist grid lines
- AdvanceTrac with Roll Stability Control (RSC)
- Trailer sway control
- Some models are equipped with additional Ford Co-Pilot360 features.

comfortably with superior performance in several areas but may not be quite as capable in other areas compared to some solid-front-axle competitors.

Comparing the top-of-the-line Bronco to the Jeep Wrangler provides insight into the key features and performance of the two vehicles. I excluded the Bronco Raptor and the Wrangler 392 because they are higher-priced specialty vehicles (not that the Wildtrak and Rubicon are low cost).

The sixth-generation Bronco's main competitor is the Jeep Wrangler JL. Here is a price comparison of the 2023 models:

2023 Bronco versus Wrangler Price Comparison			
Ford Bronco (Four Door)	Price	Jeep Wrangler (Four Door)	Price
Base	$35,200	Sport	$35,590
Big Bend	$37,880	Willys Sport	$38,585
Black Diamond	$40,045	Sport S	$38,395
		Sport Altitude	$41,885
Outer Banks	$43,450	Freedom	$42,085
		Willys	$42,585
Badlands	$46,590	Sahara	$46,020
Wildtrak	$51,225	Rubicon	$47,890
Everglades	$53,000	Sahara Altitude	$50,720
		High Alt	$55,115
Raptor	$77,300	Rubicon Xtreme Recon	$66,300
		Rubicon 392	$82,495

The base-model Bronco provides good off-road capability, especially when equipped with the optional Sasquatch package. (Photo Courtesy Ford Motor Company)

The original first-generation Bronco was one of the most capable off-roader vehicles of all time, starting with the 1966 model year. With the mighty small-block V-8 engine and a solid front axle, the first-generation Bronco was arguably the best off-road vehicle of the era. While the sixth-generation Bronco looks modern, many of the design features pay tribute to the heritage of the original Bronco, including the peaked front fenders. (Photo Courtesy Ford Motor Company)

The new Bronco models excel in the desert. With the top off and the doors removed, the Bronco Wildtrak with the Sasquatch package (only standard on the Wildtrak and Heritage models and optional on all other models) tackles the sand dunes with ease. (Photo Courtesy Ford Motor Company)

Bronco Wildtrak versus Wrangler Rubicon (Xtreme Recon Package)		
	Bronco Wildtrak	**Jeep Rubicon**
Overall Width without Mirrors	79.5 inches	75.9 inches
Height	77.8 inches	73.6 inches
Wheelbase	116.1 inches	118.4 inches
Ground Clearance	11.51 inches	10.8 inches
Angle of Approach	43.2 degrees	49 degrees
Angle of Departure	37.5 degrees	42 degrees
Breakover Angle	30.8 degrees	8 degrees
Maximum Tow Capacity	3,500 pounds	3,500 pounds
Transmission Gear Ratios (auto)	First: 4.741:1	First: 4.71:1
	Second: 2.997:1	Second: 3.1:1
	Third: 2.149:1	Third: 2.10:1
	Fourth: 1.769:1	Fourth: 1.67:1
	Fifth: 1.521:1	Fifth: 1.28:1
	Sixth: 1.275:1	Sixth: 100:1
	Seventh: 1.000:1	Seventh: 0.84:1
	Eighth: 0.853:1	Eighth: 0.67:1
	Ninth: 0.689:1	
	Tenth: 0.636:1	
Shocks	3.1-inch Fox internal bypass (external reservoir)	Fox high-pressure gas (monotube)
Electric Front Sway-Bar Disconnect	No	Yes
Axle Ratio	4.7:1	4.88:1
Low-Range Transfer-Case Ratio	3.0:1	4.0:1
Crawl Ratio	68.7	91.7 (85.9 with 4.46 axle ratio)
Horsepower	330	285
Torque	415	260
Power to Weight Ratio	14.4	15.6
Price (approx.)	$63,020.00	$66,300.00

Trim Level	Available G.O.A.T. Modes
Base	Normal, Eco, Sport, Slippery, and Sand/Snow
Big Bend	Normal, Eco, Sport, Slippery, Sand/Snow, and Mud/Ruts
Outer Banks	Normal, Eco, Sport, Slippery, Sand/Snow, and Mud/Ruts
Wildtrak	Normal, Eco, Sport, Slippery, Sand/Snow, and Mud/Ruts
Black Diamond	Normal, Eco, Sport, Slippery, Sand/Snow, Mud/Ruts, and Rock Crawl
Badland	Normal, Eco, Slippery, Sand/Snow, Mud/Ruts, Rock Crawl, and Baja
Everglades	Normal, Eco, Sport, Slippery, Sand/Snow, Mud/Ruts, and Rock Crawl
Heritage	Normal, Eco, Sport, Slippery, and Sand/Snow
Heritage Limited	Normal, Eco, Sport, Slippery, Sand/Snow, Mud/Ruts, and Rock Crawl
Raptor	Normal, Sport, Slippery, Tow-Haul, Rock Crawl, and Baja

2023 Bronco G.O.A.T. Modes

Nine G.O.A.T. modes were created for the 2023 Bronco: Normal, Eco, Sport, Slippery, Sand/Snow, Mud/Ruts, Rock Crawl, Baja, and Tow-Haul.

Available as a default mode on all Bronco trims, the Normal mode is perfect for everyday driving and provides an

The Bronco Wildtrak, with the standard Sasquatch package, HOSS 3.0 suspension, and engine upgrades, shines on desert terrain as well as in snowy conditions. (Photo Courtesy Ford Motor Company)

The Ford Bronco created a serious challenge to the Jeep Wrangler lineup. Each vehicle performs exceptionally well off-road. The Bronco Wildtrak's independent front suspension holds a slight edge in the rolling and rutted desert terrain, but the Jeep Wrangler Rubicon, with its solid-front-axle setup, takes on the rocks more easily. (Photo Courtesy Stellantis)

The design of the Bronco Badlands model favors the rough terrain of rocky areas. The Badlands features a front sway-bar disconnect, which is not available on other models even as an option. With the optional Sasquatch package, the Badlands is a formidable rock crawler in stock trim on all but the most extreme rock-crawling trails. (Photo Courtesy Ford Motor Company)

The Bronco's G.O.A.T modes are available based on the trim level. This Bronco is in "Slippery" mode.

The electronics on the sixth-generation Broncos are state of the art. The G.O.A.T. modes alter computer settings for several different types of conditions and terrain. Different Bronco models utilize a varying range of G.O.A.T. modes.

The Trail Control feature maintains the maximum speed of the Bronco at low speeds (and even lower speeds while using the system in reverse). Use the steering wheel to control direction. The speed is set with the arrows on the steering wheel and the dash screen readout. Once your speed is set, the vehicle applies power to all four wheels to keep driving at the desired speed. You only have to steer.

The camera system on the Bronco provides several views, including the birds-eye view next to the forward trail view. The bird's-eye view is accomplished by stitching multiple camera images together (including fisheye cameras under the side mirrors) and merging them together to form one image. The vehicle in the image is actually a graphic overlay (not your real vehicle), so if you left your coffee cup on the roof, it would not appear on the screen.

The cockpit layout on the Bronco features a large screen with many useful features. The yellow-trimmed grab handle is not positioned for effective support for the passenger. The lack of a grab bar below the glove-compartment door is curious.

The shifter layout is good with the exception of the manual shift mode control, which uses a "+/-" toggle switch on the side of the shifter knob. It feels somewhat awkward and takes time to get used to.

The Trail Control feature maintains the maximum speed of the Bronco at low speeds (and even lower speeds while using the system in reverse). Use the steering wheel to control direction. The speed is set with the arrows on the steering wheel and the dash screen readout. Once your speed is set, the vehicle applies power to all four wheels to keep driving at the desired speed. You only have to steer.

optimal balance among performance, practicality, and comfort.

By tuning the engine for maximum fuel efficiency, the Eco mode decreases fuel consumption and improves the driving range. This mode is ideal for city and highway driving, where there is no need for differential locks or enhanced throttle response.

With improved performance, handling, and throttle response, the Sport mode is engineered for those who like to have a sportier, more exhilarating drive. The steering becomes more stiff and nimble, and the powertrain holds onto lower gears for a longer amount of time, resulting in instant power delivery and rapid acceleration.

The Slippery mode should be your first choice when driving on snow or ice-covered roads. It slows the throttle response and optimizes gear shifts to tackle wet and slippery surfaces. In addition, traction and stability controls are made more restrictive to provide better control.

The Sand/Snow mode comes in handy while traversing loose surfaces, such as deep sand or snow. This mode engages the four-wheel drive lock, improves braking performance, and amplifies engine sound.

With the assistance of the Mud/Ruts mode, the Bronco can easily navigate muddy, rutted, or uneven terrain. In this mode, the four-wheel drive lock gets engaged, transmitting the power to all four wheels evenly. Moreover, the traction and stability control allows for more momentum-maintaining wheelspin. So, for those who like to go mudding (or those who despise getting trapped in mud), the Mud/Ruts mode is the most suitable choice.

For adventure lovers who aren't scared of conquering challenging rocks in their off-road pursuits, nothing beats the Rock Crawl mode. It engages the rear differential and four-wheel drive locks while also turning on the front trail camera at low speeds so that you can see the approaching objects more clearly.

The Baja mode is the ultimate driving mode for high-speed off-roading, especially on loose terrain, such as sand. In this setting, the suspension, throttle response, and torque delivery are all optimized for extreme off-road performance.

The Bronco Raptor features an exclusive Tow/Haul mode, which allows it to pull up to 4,500 pounds. For enhanced towing power, the upshifts take place at higher speeds than normal, and the frequency of gear shifts are reduced. Moreover, engine braking is applied while descending steep slopes.

Model Details

Below is a list of the various models with features relative to off-road performance:

2024 Bronco Big Bend
- Trail Control (requires 10-speed transmission) (available option)
- Trail Turn Assist (requires 10-speed transmission) (available option)
- Trail 1-Pedal Drive (requires 2.7L or 3.0L engine and 10-speed auto) (available option)
- High-Performance Off-Road Stability Suspension (HOSS) 1.0 system
- 4x4 with Part-Time Selectable Engagement
- HOSS 2.0 system (with Bilstein position-sensitive damper [PSD] shock absorbers and high-clearance ride height) (available option)
- Advanced 4x4 with automatic on-demand engagement (available option)
- Electronic locking rear axle (available option)
- Electronic locking front and rear axle (available option)
- Sasquatch package (available option)

2024 Bronco Black Diamond
- Trail Control (requires 10-speed transmission) (available option)
- Trail Turn Assist (requires 10-speed transmission) (available option)
- HOSS 1.0 system
- 4x4 with part-time selectable engagement
- Electronic locking rear axle
- HOSS 2.0 system (with Bilstein position-sensitive dampers (PSDs), and high-clearance ride height) (available option)
- Advanced 4x4 with automatic on-demand engagement (available option)
- Electronic locking front and rear axle (available option)
- Sasquatch package (available option)
- Auxiliary switches with pre-run accessory wires (located in overhead console with front map lights)

The Bronco Big Bend model features 32-inch Bridgestone Dueler A/T tires, making it a very good off-roader on easy to moderate trails in stock form. (Photo Courtesy Ford Motor Company)

Ford dealerships offer many dealer-installed options, including rooftop crossbars, a cargo basket and roof light bars, cowl lights, a winch bumper mount and winch, and a four-door pull-out tailgate. (Photo Courtesy Ford Motor Company)

2024 Bronco Outer Banks

- Trail 1-Pedal Drive (requires 2.7L or 3.0L engine and 10-speed auto) (available option)
- 360-degree camera (available option)

2024 Bronco Badlands

- Trail Control (requires 10-speed transmission) (available option)
- Trail Turn Assist (requires 10-speed transmission) (available option)
- Trail 1-Pedal Drive (requires 2.7L or 3.0L engine and 10-speed auto) (available option)
- 360-degree camera (available option)
- HOSS 2.0 system (with Bilstein PSDs and high-clearance ride height) (available option)
- Advanced 4x4 with automatic on-demand engagement
- Electronic-locking front and rear axle
- Trail Control (requires 10-speed transmission) (available option)
- Trail Turn Assist (requires 10-speed transmission) (available option)
- Trail 1-Pedal Drive (requires 2.7L or 3.0L engine and 10-speed auto) (available option)

2024 Bronco Wildtrak

- 360-degree camera (available option)
- HOSS 3.0 system (with Fox Internal Bypass Dampers) (high-clearance ride height)
- Ford Performance severe-duty steering rack and tie-rod ends;

The Outer Banks model offers additional features, including the High Performance Off-Road Stability Suspension (HOSS) 2.0 System with Bilstein PSD shock absorbers. (Photo Courtesy Ford Motor Company)

The Bronco Badlands offers features including the front sway-bar disconnect, making it the best choice for moderate to difficult rock-crawling trails. (Photo Courtesy Ford Motor Company)

front steel bumper with fog lamps

- Advanced 4x4 with automatic on-demand engagement
- Electronic locking rear axle
- Electronic locking front and rear axle
- Sasquatch package is standard on the Wildtrak

2024 Bronco Everglades

- HOSS 2.0 system (with Bilstein PSDs and high-clearance ride height)
- Advanced 4x4 with automatic on-demand engagement
- Electronic locking front and rear axle
- Trail Control (requires 10-speed transmission)
- Trail Turn Assist (requires 10-speed transmission)
- Hill Start Assist
- Sasquatch package
- HOSS 2.0 system (with Bilstein PSDs and high-clearance ride height)
- Advanced 4x4 with automatic on-demand engagement
- Electronic locking front and rear axle
- Sasquatch package

2024 Bronco Raptor

- HOSS 4.0 system (with Fox live-valve 3.1 internal-bypass semi-active dampers)
- Advanced 4x4 with automatic on-demand engagement
- Electronic locking front and rear axles
- Front stabilizer-bar disconnect

All of the original equipment tires that are listed are off-road tires, except for the base-model Bridgestone Dueler H/T. None of the tires that come on any Bronco would make my list for the most capable

The premiere desert off-roader in the Bronco lineup is the Wildtrak. Among the extensive list of features are the HOSS 3.0 package with Fox internal-bypass dampers, a high-clearance ride height, Ford Performance severe-duty steering rack and tie-rod ends, a front steel bumper with fog lamps, and 35-inch-diameter tires on 17-inch alloy wheels. Surprisingly, the electric front sway-bar disconnect is not available, requiring the installation of an aftermarket sway-bar disconnect. (Photo Courtesy Ford Motor Company)

The Everglades version offers more luxury features but does come equipped with 35-inch-diameter tires on 17-inch alloy wheels. (Photo Courtesy Ford Motor Company)

The Bronco Raptor offers many standard features, making it the premier off-road vehicle in the Bronco lineup—along with a matching price tag. The Raptor is very wide, which improves stability laterally in rough terrain but limits its ability to navigate the tight quarters on some trails. (Photo Courtesy Ford Motor Company)

Desert terrain allows the Bronco Raptor to shine. The HOSS 4.0 with Fox 3.1 live-valve, internal-bypass, semi-active dampers make the Raptor exceptional in the undulating desert environment. (Photo Courtesy Ford Motor Company)

The Goodyear Territory mud-terrain tires on the Bronco Wildtrak seriously limit the performance of the Wildtrak anytime the surface is even remotely slippery. Locations on familiar trails that I have never used lockers on a 4x4 vehicle required the use of at least the rear locker to successfully negotiate the hill or obstacle, even with the front sway-bar disconnect and the tire pressures set to a low 12 psi.

Ford Bronco Tire Specifications					
Trim	Tire Size	Tire Make & Model	Wheel Type	Tire Diameter (inches)	Wheel Size (inches)
Base	255/70	Bridgestone Dueler H/T	Steel	30	16
Big Bend	255/75	Bridgestone Dueler A/T RH-S	Aluminum	32	17
Outer Banks	255/70	Bridgestone Dueler A/T RH-S	Aluminum	32	18
Black Diamond	265/70	General Grabber A/T	Steel	32	17
Badlands	285/70	BFGoodrich All-Terrain T/A KO2 & Goodyear Territory	Aluminum	33	17
Wildtrak	315/70	Goodyear Territory	Aluminum	35	17
First Edition	315/70	Goodyear Territory	Aluminum	35	17
Everglades	315/70	Goodyear Territory	Alloy	35	17
Heritage Limited 35-Edition	315/70	Goodyear Territory	Aluminum	35	17
Sasquatch Package	315/70	Goodyear Territory	Aluminum	35	17
Bronco Raptor	315/80	BFGoodrich All-Terrain T/A KO2	Alloy	37	17

off-road tires (and the Trails 411 team has tested all of these tires). Any of the off-road (all-terrain [A/T], mud-terrain [M/T] and rugged-terrain [R/T]) tires from Hankook, Mickey Thompson, Nexen, Nitto, Falken, etc., provide superior off-road performance when compared to the original equipment tires on the Bronco models (see chapter 3 for more tire information).

Sasquatch Package

The Sasquatch Package includes 35-inch tires, 17-inch beadlock-capable wheels, electronic-locking front and rear differentials, and high-clearance fender flares. The Sasquatch package is available on all Bronco models except the Raptor, which has many similar features, and it is standard equipment on the Wildtrak and Heritage models. The cost for the Sasquatch package is about $6,000.

Some people question the value of the Sasquatch package. The ability to order a model that includes the Sasquatch package or to add it to any other non-Raptor model sets the Bronco lineup apart from other off-road-capable vehicles. Anyone considering any model of Bronco should include the Sasquatch package in the build.

On the surface, any 4x4 vehicle can travel off-road. I recently helped a student learn to navigate some challenging sections of an easy trail in a Big Bend Bronco Sport. The Big Bend Bronco Sport uses small tires and relies on electronics for four-wheel drive and other off-road features. The tires are only 29 inches tall, leaving little ground clearance. The Bronco Sport not only surprised me but it also made it through a few difficult spots. Was it easy? No. Did it push the Bronco Sport to its limits? Yes.

Dirt roads and off-road trails, especially in the Southwest and on the West Coast have deteriorated considerably over the last decade, resulting in heavily rutted roads, exposed rocks, and generally tougher terrain. Several factors have contributed to this deterioration: more vehicles traveling off-road, severe weather, lack of adequate road maintenance by land managers, the increased use of side-by-sides, and the exploding popularity of overlanding.

The Sasquatch package on any model of Bronco elevates the capability of the vehicle to easily handle the deteriorating conditions of off-road trail systems. More lift, larger off-road tires, and other off-road features on the Sasquatch package reduce the risk of vehicle damage and make getting stuck considerably less likely. Unless you know from personal experience (or from reliable sources) that the terrain is easy to explore, go with the Sasquatch package for moderate to difficult–rated trails.

The Sasquatch package provides several features, improving the off-road capabilities for all models (standard on the Wildtrak and Heritage and optional on all other models). The tires on the Wildtrak limit off-road performance.

Other Bronco Electronic Controls

When encountering very tight turns at low speeds and using considerable steering input, flip the Trail Turn Assist button to easily make multipoint turns. The assist locks the inside rear tire, causing it to slide, which substantially reduces the turning radius. This is an unusual feature that is very handy and a lot of fun to use.

The Trail Control feature works like cruise control for low-speed off-road driving.

The 1-Pedal Drive feature, once set at a given speed, allows acceleration by using the throttle pedal, but when the throttle is released, the Bronco will reduce speed back to the preset speed without using the brake pedal.

When the Trail Turn Assist feature is engaged, it locks the inside rear tire in a tight turn to virtually eliminate the need for multipoint turns. It's a very useful feature.

2023 BRONCO WILDTRAK TWO-DOOR OFF-ROAD TEST

Ford hit a home run with the sixth-generation Bronco. The Bronco lineup provides a variety of choices for many levels of users—from a daily driver to a capable trail rig and an excellent overlanding vehicle. The Bronco that was used for this chapter's testing was the two-door Bronco Wildtrak, which is touted as the best version for desert running. The Bronco Wildtrak features the Sasquatch package, which includes the HOSS 3.0 package with Fox internal-bypass dampers, a high-clearance ride height, Ford Performance severe-duty steering rack and tie-rod ends, and front steel bumper with fog lamps.

Surprisingly, the Wildtrak does not come with the front stabilizer-bar (sway-bar) disconnect, nor is it an available option. Add the 35-inch tires and optional turbo 2.7L EcoBoost V-6 engine and the 10-speed automatic transmission, and the Bronco becomes a formidable on- and off-road SUV.

While the test was primarily focused on off-road performance, highway performance and the extensive list of electronic and comfort

The Trails 411 team, including the author, had the opportunity to test the Ford Bronco Wildtrak two-door model on the trails near Big Bear Lake and Cougar Buttes in California.

The tie-rods on the Bronco take a beating and are prone to failure, even with the upgraded tie-rods and steering rack on the Wildtrak model. Steering failure on the trail results in a difficult vehicle recovery.

One of the best features on the Bronco Wildtrak is the braking system. I put the excellent brakes to the test on the steep downhill section on California Highway 18 from Big Bear to Cougar Buttes.

features is worth noting. The most notable feature pins you back in the seat when the 330 hp and 400 ft-lbs of torque kicks in. The acceleration is stunning—at least after the turbo lag disappears. With a low-speed rolling start and then applying full throttle, turbo lag is notable. However, when the turbo spools up, acceleration is great. Towing capacity tops out at 3,500 pounds, which seems a little low given the engine power and the substantial suspension.

Off-road, the Bronco Wildtrak brakes performed really well on steep descents, even when not using the hill-descent control. At very low speeds, the brakes are a little touchy, especially when rock crawling.

Ride quality feels very comfortable on the less-than-smooth roads in Southern California. Handling on the highway, especially on the twists and turns of the local mountain roads, instills confidence. It provides good stability, excellent steering feel, and good cornering capability. This is all enhanced by the HOSS 3.0 package with Fox internal-bypass dampers.

Brakes take a beating on the steep downhill, twisty sections of California Highway 18 on the backside of the city of Big Bear. The big brakes on the Bronco Wildtrak provided

excellent stopping power when slowing the beast from higher speeds to negotiate some of the tight turns and hairpin corners on the test route. While slowing quickly for speeds in the 50-mph range to negotiate much slower corners, the Bronco's brakes faded noticeably. While not affecting deceleration, increased pedal pressure was necessary to reduce speed for the fast-approaching corners. Few drivers will experience brake fade in normal or even fairly aggressive driving situations.

Without a doubt, the 12-inch LCD touchscreen display with Swipe Capability and Enhanced Voice Rec-

ognition and the 12-inch dash gauge instrument cluster exceed expectations. During the week that the Bronco Wildtrak was driven, it was a challenge to utilize even a portion of the myriad of features that are available with this technology.

The most impressive features include the 360-degree camera with off-road views. Front, rear, and mirror-mounted cameras provide several views that are helpful for off-road driving. The full bird's-eye view around the vehicle is like having a drone hovering 20 feet above. This can be very helpful in tight quarters.

The 12-inch touch screen on the Bronco dash provides excellent visibility and is easy to access. The camera system is exceptional, although the high quality and myriad of features can be distracting.

The forward-facing trail cam and the overhead bird's-eye view feature makes navigating tight spots and parking a breeze. Note that the graphic overlay does not match the color of the test vehicle.

2023 Ford Bronco Wildtrak Standard Equipment

To fully appreciate the extent of the Bronco sixth-generation features, here is a list of standard equipment on the Bronco Wildtrak:

Mechanical
- Engine: 2.7L EcoBoost V-6 (including electric brake boost)
- Transmission: 10-speed automatic

The Wildtrak hood graphics and badging add a nice graphic touch.

(including Trail Control, Trail Turn Assist, and Trail 1-Pedal driving)
- Axle ratio: 4.7:1
- Gross vehicle weight rating (GVWR): 6,160 pounds
- 50-state emissions system
- Engine auto stop/start feature
- Transmission with driver-selectable mode, sequential

The Bronco Hero switches activate several of the Bronco's off-road features. From left to right on the Wildtrak are the front and rear differential locks, Trail Turn Assist, electronic stability control, and the hazard lights. When the front and rear differential locks are activated, the available electronic-locking front and rear differential locks the wheels on each axle to optimize traction and improve off-road performance. Trail Turn Assist reduces the turning radius of the vehicle by applying the brakes to the inside rear wheel in low-speed, high-steering-angle maneuvers. This gives the vehicle the ability to get through tight bends more easily. Electronic stability control activates when wheel slip is detected, and the slipping wheel will get the brakes applied so that the engine power is delivered to both wheels.

The central dial uses push buttons to select drive modes. The center button engages Trail Assist, and the dial rotates to engage the G.O.A.T. modes.

shift control, and oil cooler
- Electronic transfer case
- Part- and full-time four-wheel drive
- Driver-selectable front locking differential
- Driver-selectable rear locking differential
- 80-amp/hr 800-cold cranking amp (CCA) maintenance-free battery with rundown protection

The center console houses the shift lever, which includes manual shift mode on the 10-speed automatic transmission. The toggle switch on the driver side of the shift knob controls up and down shifting in manual mode. Storage is good. The grab handle is oddly placed.

The sound system and climate controls are easily accessed on the central dash. The dual temperature controls provide customized temperature zones.

The driver analog speedometer is easy to read. The large dash screen offers several options, providing a wealth of information. The screen pages are easily scrolled with controls on the steering wheel.

- Regenerative 250-amp alternator
- Towing equipment, including trailer sway control
- Three skid plates
- 1,225-pound maximum payload
- Front anti-roll bar
- Off-road suspension
- Fox Racing remote-reservoir shock absorbers
- Electric power-assist steering
- Single stainless-steel exhaust
- 20.8-gallon fuel tank
- Auto locking hubs
- Short- and long-arm front suspension with coil springs
- Solid-axle rear suspension with coil springs
- Brakes with front and rear vented discs, brake assist, hill-hold control, and electric parking brake
- Up-fitter switches

Exterior
- Wheels: 17-inch black high gloss–painted aluminum, including: black beauty ring and beadlock-capable wheels

- Tires: LT315/70R17 mud-terrain, including full-size spare tire with tire-pressure monitoring system (TPMS) sensors
- Aluminum spare wheel
- Spare tire mounted outside rear
- Clearcoat paint with decal
- Black front bumper with two tow hooks

When manual shift mode is used on the 10-speed automatic transmission, the gear selection is made with a toggle switch on the shift knob. This unusual way to shift takes some time to use smoothly, but once the driver is acclimated to the location and the toggle switch action, shifting is easy.

- Black rear step bumper with one tow hook
- Black fender flares
- Black side window trim
- Black door handles
- Black power heated side mirrors (with convex spotter and manual folding)
- Removable rear window
- Variable intermittent wipers
- Deep tinted glass
- Fully galvanized steel panels
- Black grille
- Manual convertible top with fixed roll-over protection
- Conventional rear cargo access
- Tailgate/rear door lock included with power door locks
- Ford Co-Pilot360: auto lamp on/off aero-composite LED auto low/high beam daytime running lights preference setting headlamps with delay off
- Headlights-automatic high beams
- Front fog lamps
- LED brake lights

Entertainment
- Radio: AM/FM stereo—seven speakers (including subwoofer)
- Radio with seek-scan, clock, speed-compensated volume control, steering-wheel controls, and radio data system
- Streaming audio
- Fixed antenna
- Sirius XM Radio with 360L
- Two LCD monitors in the front
- Turn-by-turn navigation directions

Interior
- Driver's seat
- Passenger's seat
- 60/40 folding split bench; front-facing, manual-reclining, fold-forward-seatback cloth rear seat

- Manual tilt/telescoping steering column
- Gauges: speedometer, odometer, voltmeter, coolant temperature, tachometer, inclinometer, trip odometer, and trip computer
- Power rear windows and removable third-row windows
- Leather/metal-look steering wheel
- Front cupholder
- Rear cupholder
- Compass
- Remote keyless entry with integrated key transmitter, illuminated entry, illuminated ignition switch, and panic button
- Proximity key for doors and push-button start
- Cruise control with steering-wheel controls
- HVAC (including under-seat ducts)
- Dual-zone front automatic air conditioning
- Locking glove box
- Driver footrest
- Leather/metal-look gear shifter material
- Interior trim (including metal-look door-panel insert and metal-look interior accents)
- Heated cloth bucket seats (including six-way manual driver and passenger seats with fore/aft, up/down, and recline adjustments)
- Day/night auto-dimming rear-view mirror
- Driver and passenger visor vanity mirrors (with driver and passenger illumination, driver and passenger auxiliary mirror)
- Full floor console (with locking storage, mini overhead console, and three 12V DC power outlets)
- Front map lights
- Fade-to-off interior lighting
- Carpet floor trim
- Full carpet floor covering (including carpet front and rear floor mats)
- Cargo space lights
- Smart-device remote engine start
- Tracker system
- Key frequency-operated button (FOB) controls (including remote engine start)
- Connected navigation
- Dashboard storage, driver/passenger and rear door bins and second-row under-seat storage
- Power first-row windows with driver and passenger one-touch up/down
- Delayed accessory power
- Power door locks with auto-lock feature
- Systems monitor
- Redundant digital speedometer
- Trip computer
- Outside temperature gauge
- Digital/analog appearance
- Seats with cloth back material
- Manual adjustable front head restraints and foldable rear head restraints
- Front center armrest
- Two seatback storage pockets
- Perimeter alarm
- Immobilizer
- Air filtration
- Three 12V DC power outlets

Safety
- ABS and driveline traction control
- Side impact beams
- Dual-stage driver and passenger seat-mounted side airbags
- Collision mitigation (front)
- Reverse-sensing system rear parking sensors
- Ford Co-Pilot360: blind-spot information system (BLIS) blind spot
- Ford Co-Pilot360: pre-collision assist (with pedestrian detection)

- Ford Co-Pilot360: cross-traffic alert
- Lane-keeping alert, lane-keeping assist
- Lane-departure alert, lane-departure warning
- Driver monitoring-alert
- Dual-stage driver and passenger front airbags
- Safety canopy system curtain first- and second-row airbags
- Personal safety system airbag occupancy sensor
- MyKey System (including top-speed limiter, audio-volume limiter, early low-fuel warning, programmable sound chimes, and belt-minder with audio mute)
- Rear child safety locks
- Outboard front lap and shoulder safety belts (including rear center three-point harness and pretensioners
- Back-up camera

In addition to the extensive list of standard features and factory

The Bronco's engine is well protected with a stout sheet-metal skid plate.

options, a long list of dealer-installed options is also available. Many of these options provide desirable features for general off-roading and especially for the overlanding enthusiast.

Dealer-Installed Options
- Wheel-lock kit
- On-road assistance kit
- Body armor (protective moldings)
- Off-road assistance kit
- Second-row panel roof-bag storage
- Tailgate table
- Mesh shade top
- Retractable full-twill soft top
- Retractable twill front row soft top
- Soft-canvas bimini top
- Tube doors (four-door)
- Cargo-area rug
- Soft tonneau cover
- Cargo net kit
- Console lock box (safe deposit)
- First-aid kit

The beadlock-capable wheels are both attractive and useful for off-road adventures when tire pressures are lowered to ideal levels. The Goodyear Territory tires left much to be desired in most off-road situations, even when aired down to 12 psi. Overall off-road traction was generally poor, hurting the Wildtrak's off-road performance. (Photo Courtesy Ford Motor Company)

The front bumper on the Wildtrak model is both attractive and strong. The steel bumper features fog lights and very substantial D-ring shackles for emergency recoveries. The lower pan is a sheet-metal skid plate (unlike many vehicles with a plastic pan), which protects the steering. The unique headlight design is distinctive and provides good nighttime lighting. (Photo Courtesy Ford Motor Company)

The Bronco rear tire carrier swings out with the tailgate, making opening and closing very easy. The steel rear bumper provides good protection. However, the muffler is exposed and prone to trail damage.

Axle articulation is pretty good on the Wildtrak with the front sway-bar disconnected, which I did by unbolting the sway-bar links from the lower control arms. The lack of the electric sway-bar disconnect that is found on the Bronco Badlands model is curious, and the lack of any rocker-panel protection is also odd.

The Bronco Wildtrak window sticker lists all of the features and options on the test rig from Ford. The price tag is more than $62,000.

Off-Road Testing

The Bronco Wildtrak is positioned in the Bronco lineup as the optimal desert off-roader. Of course, the tests in this book occurred in the desert at Cougar Buttes, which is part of the Johnson Valley Off-Highway Vehicle Recreation Area and home to the King of the Hammers race. Testing also occurred in the Big Bear Lake area, which is home to more than 300 miles of off-road trails that range from mild to extreme. Testing included hill climbs and descents, ruts, and moderate rock crawling at the training area near the Rose Mine. There are some good rolling bumps and ruts for testing the higher-speed capabilities of the Bronco Wildtrak HOSS 3.0 suspension with the Fox shocks. In the desert, the suspension was tested on the whoops that dominate most of the roads in the area as well as washboard sections, sand, and some rocky areas that find the limits of breakover, approach and departure angles, and articulation.

So, how did the Bronco Wildtrak fair? Stay tuned!

For the off-road testing, the front sway (stabilizer) bar was disconnected, even though the Bronco Wildtrak does not come with a front sway-bar disconnect. The sway-bar links were unbolted from the lower control arm and zip tied out of harm's way. At the time, the front electric sway-bar disconnect was only

The Wildtrak features the Trail Turn Assist feature, which is activated by a Hero switch on the dashboard. This feature was handy when negotiating tight turns in close quarters. The turning radius is made much smaller by locking the inside rear tire in tight turns.

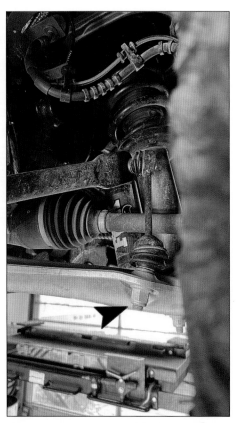

By removing the nut (black arrow) that attaches the front sway bar link to the front lower control arm, I disconnected the front sway bar, allowing for maximum front articulation. After disconnecting the sway-bar link, the link was zip tied to the sway-bar arm.

available on the Badlands, First Edition, and Raptor models.

However, aftermarket sway-bar disconnects are available for the Bronco. Disconnecting the sway bar assured that maximum axle articulation could occur. Tire pressure on the Goodyear Territory 35-inch (LT315/70R17) mud-terrain tires was set at 12 psi. This allowed maximum tire sidewall flex while minimizing possible damage to the beadlock-capable wheels.

Sand

The Bronco Wildtrak thrives on sand. The Goodyear Territory tires are not the best in sand, but with G.O.A.T. Sand mode engaged (which engages the rear locker), the Bronco performed well. Lower tire pressures and a more suitable tire would really bring the Bronco to life in the sand. The independent front suspension on the Bronco does not seem to improve sand performance.

Rolling Bumps and Ruts

The HOSS 3.0 package on the Wildtrak version shines in the high-speed bumps. The damping in the shocks is ideal for controlling and stabilizing the Bronco. The Wildtrak platform glides over the big, higher-speed bumps and ruts with ease, which provides a very secure feel.

The tire pressures on the Goodyear Territory tires on the test rig were lowered to 12 psi. This increased tire traction on granite rocks but was still not up to the standard of other off-road tires I have tested. Overall traction was poor and hurt the performance of the Bronco during testing. I limited some tests due to the poor lateral traction that allowed the Bronco to slide and shift sideways when crawling. Without good traction laterally and the lack of rock sliders, I opted to avoid situations where sliding sideways off rocks could damage the rocker panels.

With the G.O.A.T. Sand mode engaged, the rear locker is on. This makes driving in the sand a breeze, which is quite abundant in the Cougar Buttes area of Johnson Valley.

The Bronco works well on rutted road terrain.

Washboard Roads

The Wildtrak handles washboard sections well if the tire pressures are reduced and speed is maintained where possible. Again, the HOSS 3.0 package with Fox internal-bypass dampers makes a big difference. How does this compare to off-road vehicles equipped with solid front axles? If a solid-front-axle rig is equipped

The Wildtrak provides good sideways stability on side slopes.

The HOSS 3.0 suspension on the Bronco Wildtrak handles rough terrain, providing good articulation and a smooth ride.

The Goodyear Territory mud-terrain tires on the Wildtrak offer adequate traction on loose dirt, but when the terrain becomes more inclined, the lack of tire traction affects the performance.

With the front sway bar disconnected on the Wildtrak, articulation on undulating ruts is good (no tire lifting) when a good line is used by the driver.

While straddling ruts parallel to the direction of travel is preferred, the Wildtrak has excellent suspension with the HOSS 3.0 package to handing driving with the tires placed in the ruts.

with shocks that are equivalent to the Fox internal-bypass shocks, there is very little difference. You can feel the slight improvement with the independent front suspension, but the solid rear axle on the Bronco reacts in the same manner as any solid-axle vehicle. The testing team determined that the improvement with the Bronco Wildtrak was about 10 percent.

Whoops

No stock 4x4 vehicle is good in the whoops! Unless a vehicle has 20-plus inches of travel and extreme shock absorbers, the ride is not pleasant. So, does the Bronco's independent front suspension help? Yes. However, with a solid-front-axle vehicle that is equipped with the equivalent shocks, the testing team's consensus is about a 10-percent

improvement over the solid-axle counterpart.

Hill Climbs

The Bronco's hill climbing test was disappointing. At the testing grounds and training area, I have driven dozens of vehicles up a 22-degree rutted slope. Students have mastered the hill in many other rigs (stock and modified). Testing took

Carrying moderate speed over bumps showcases the HOSS 3.0 suspension on the Bronco Wildtrak. A difference between the front and rear damping is noticeable with the independent front suspension and a solid rear axle.

to complete the climb, stopping in a cloud of wheelspin-induced dust. After backing down the slope and engaging the lockers, the Bronco had no difficulty climbing the slope. Keep in mind that the front stabilizer bar was disconnected, although that should not have made a difference.

I have no doubt that the Bronco is much more capable than what was shown on this and other climbs. While the shorter-wheelbase two-door model may have played a minor role in the problem, the true culprit was the Goodyear Territory tires. Even aired down to 12 psi, the tires did not have the grip needed to make it to the top. There is no question that the Bronco would have easily made

place on a stock Jeep Wrangler JLU Sport S with no lockers on the factory 31-inch Bridgestone all-terrain tires. The Jeep and every other vehicle that has been tested (including student vehicles) have never needed lockers to negotiate the hill climb. Frankly, I was surprised when the Bronco failed

Climbing diagonally was not an issue for the Bronco, but the Goodyear Territory tires struggled.

While the Bronco made this climb, which is steeper than it appears in the photo, wheelspin was an issue without at least the rear locker engaged.

The Bronco Wildtrak required the rear locker to negotiate this 22-degree climb on loose dirt with some deep ruts.

At the apex of the climb, the front tires on the Wildtrak gained some traction, but the rear tires began to spin slightly.

This rocky V-notch climb presented no issues for the Wildtrak.

the ascent with better tires—and it was not just on this climb. On other climbs as well, wheelspin occurred in many locations that surprised me. I wish that I could have tested another tire on this vehicle.

Hill Descents

While the low amount of grip from the Goodyear Territory tires was an issue climbing hills, descending was much less of a problem, due in part to the excellent 4-low, first-gear crawl ratio. On steeper grades, some tire sliding was present while riding the brakes but was very manageable. Downhill braking performance proved to be acceptable.

Ruts and Bumps

Driving through ruts and bumps, especially the worsening ruts and bumps as trail systems continue to deteriorate, requires significant axle articulation. Any independent front suspension vehicle (Broncos included) cannot articulate as well as

The low-range gearing on the Wildtrak coupled with 1-Pedal Drive maintained a slow, steady speed on the rocky V-notch descent.

Dropping down a moderate 22-degree slope presented no issues for the Bronco Wildtrak. Even with the deep ruts on the descent, the HOSS 3.0 suspension with the front sway-bar disconnected kept all four tires firmly planted on the road surface.

a solid-front-axle-equipped vehicle. It's just the nature of the beast. Disconnecting the front sway (stabilizer) bar certainly helps.

The lack of articulation has two problems. First, when a tire lifts off the ground, that tire will often return back to the ground very abruptly, potentially damaging the suspension components. Given the weak tie-rods on all sixth-generation Bronco models, slamming back to the ground is not a good idea. Second, it's scary when a wheel lifts a few feet off the ground or the vehicle begins to teeter-totter. Over time, one can become accustomed to the wheel lifting, but it's not optimal. Ask the question, "Is it dangerous?" For the most part, no—unless you consider the "pucker factor" being dangerous. Even solid-front-axle vehicles can lift tires in extreme situations. While rolling or tipping over is possible, it would take an extreme situation for this to occur. Otherwise, the driver would need to react in a completely incorrect manner to induce a rollover.

Rock Crawling

The Bronco Wildtrak is not at its best on the rocks. The Badlands model with the standard electric sway-bar disconnect and the optional Sasquatch package is a much better choice for rock crawling.

While cresting the bumpy climbing, the lack of articulation on the Bronco (even with the front sway bar disconnected) caused the left front tire to lift off the ground.

Dropping into a rut while steering caused the left front tire to lift on the Bronco.

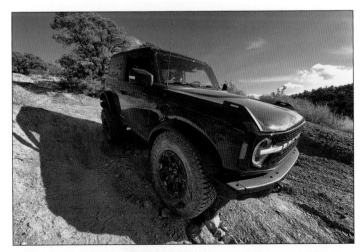

Independent front suspension is not at its best over bumps and ruts, but with the front sway bar disconnected, articulation is good with the right front tire at full bump travel and the right rear tire fully extended.

The left rear tire is up on a rock, causing the right front suspension to fully compress and the right rear to travel nearly fully extended. Good articulation is shown here.

As with any independent front suspension vehicle, the Wildtrak is prone to lifting a tire on rough, rutted sections of road.

Climbing up a rock with only the right front tire causes the right front suspension to compress, indicating good articulation with the front sway bar disconnected. The electric sway-bar disconnect is not available on the Bronco Wildtrak since it is only offered on the Badlands, Raptor, and Heritage models. While the Bronco Wildtrak is marketed as the best for desert terrain, not offering the electric front sway-bar disconnect on the Wildtrak is odd. Several aftermarket front sway-bar-disconnect systems are available.

The reduced articulation capability of the independent front suspension on the Bronco negatively affects traction, even with the front sway bar disconnected. The wheelspin during the rocky climb at the testing grounds caused the Bronco to slide sideways off the preferred line. This often resulted in more wheel lift off the ground than would be the case if the tires held laterally and if the forward grip of the tires limited or stopped wheelspin. Once again, the issue was related to the poor grip of the original-equipment tire, not on the actual capability of the Bronco.

Left-foot braking requires the braking force to be implemented smoothly. The testing crew, which includes instructors at Trails 411 Off Road training, use and teach left-foot braking, which reduces wheelspin and preloads the driveline to make breakage less likely. Even with light application of the Bronco brakes, at

Climbing up a rock with a single tire presents no problem for the Bronco.

The two-door Bronco Wildtrak has a good breakover angle for rock-crawling situations, but the lack of a rock slider is cause for concern. Our testers avoided situations in the rocks where I could damage the rocker panels. Even though the test Bronco Wildtrak was capable of crawling larger rocks, I chose to avoid them to not risk damage. Several companies offer rock sliders, including the slider steps from Rockslide Engineering.

low speed, the brakes grab a little too much, making climbing rocks and hills more difficult. While the Bronco has the 1-Pedal Drive feature that applies the brakes when the throttle pedal is released (when activated and at low speeds), the driver-controlled, left-foot braking offers better control, especially in the rocks. The 1-Pedal Drive feature works well when descending steep hills, but this feature does not allow the subtle adjustments to the brake pedal pressure that the driver is able to make with left-foot braking.

The Bronco Wildtrak with 35-inch-tall tires features a good approach angle, making rock crawling easier. The splash pan below the bumper serves as a good sheet-metal skid plate protecting the vulnerable steering components.

Maneuvering in the rocks requires good axle articulation. I was surprised by the degree of articulation on the Bronco Wildtrak with the front sway bar disconnected. An aftermarket sway-bar disconnect is a desirable upgrade.

Rocky hill climbs are not the easiest in the Wildtrak. The lack of traction, especially the limited sideways grip of the Goodyear Territory mud-terrain tires, causes the Bronco to slip sideways off rocks, altering the optimal line. This caused the Wildtrak to lift a front tire at the top of the climb. The left front raises about 18 inches off the ground, even with the front sway bar disconnected. Even with the front and rear lockers engaged, wheelspin occurred when wheelspin was not expected. Without lockers, the wheelspin was excessive and made the ascent nearly impossible.

Based on other rock-crawling experiences with the Bronco, I was certain that the Wildtrak could handle some of the sections of the Cake Walk trail in Cougar Buttes that are part of the Johnson Valley National Off-Highway Vehicle Recreation Area in Johnson Valley, California. Due to the poor tire traction of the OEM tires and a lack of protection, I declined to push the envelope too far. I would love to test the Bronco Wildtrak with better tires and more protection, such as rock sliders.

The Bronco Wildtrak performs well in the desert terrain of Cougar Buttes. The HOSS 3.0 suspension handles the bumps and ruts with ease.

Again, the aftermarket comes to the rescue. While the underside features skid plates for the engine, gas tanks, and transfer case, the transmission pan is left unprotected. Even though the pan is tucked between the frame rails, the unprotected plastic pan can be easily damaged if a sharp rock were to roll under the vehicle and puncture the pan. It has happened. Aftermarket skid plates are available.

Upgrades to Make Before Going Off-Road

Questionable Features on an Off-Road-Capable Vehicle

Several items on the stock sixth-generation Broncos, especially on the more capable models, created questions for the testing team. Most notable are the steering tie-rods. By any standard, the tie-rods are skimpy. The number of failed tie-rods on the Bronco steering system is quite amazing. Even the factory upgraded tie-rods on various packages are inadequate. Recovering a vehicle with broken steering components on the trail is difficult. A broken tie-rod on the highway is much worse.

A closely related second issue is the rack-and-pinion steering box. If a rack-support bushing becomes displaced from the rack housing, the pinion gear can become disengaged from the rack, causing a total loss of steering. Either a rack-box failure or a broken tie-rod causes steering loss. Thankfully, the Bronco aftermarket offers much stronger steering components to solve these issues (see chapter 5 for more information).

In addition, the lack of rocker-panel protection with rock sliders on the Wildtrak model is strange. The panels can be expensive

to repair and need protection even for moderate and easy trail adventures.

The lack of a sway-bar disconnect on the Wildtrak is also strange.

Critical upgrades to the Bronco Wildtrak (and other models in the Bronco lineup) improve safety, performance and vehicle protection. Here

While the steering tie-rods on any independent front suspension off-road vehicle are a weak link, the tie-rods on the Ford Broncos are more problematic than on other vehicles and have a large number of failures. Steering-system failures make for a very difficult recovery unless spares are carried. The Bronco Wildtrak has upgraded tie-rods compared to the lower-priced models, with the Bronco Raptor having even larger tie-rods. They are not adequate for anything but moderate off-roading. Even hitting a rut or bump too hard, especially while turning, can cause a tie-rod failure. The first item that I would replace is the tie-rods. Several companies, such as Fabtech, Icon Vehicle Dynamics, and SteerSmarts offer quality aftermarket tie-rods for the Bronco.

The Wildtrak provides sheet-metal skid plates for the plastic fuel tank as well as the engine and transfer case. Aftermarket full coverage steel and aluminum skid plate systems are available from several suppliers.

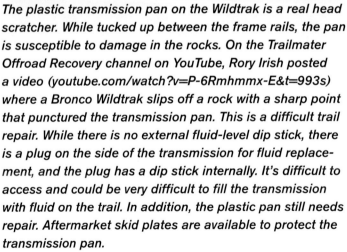

The plastic transmission pan on the Wildtrak is a real head scratcher. While tucked up between the frame rails, the pan is susceptible to damage in the rocks. On the Trailmater Offroad Recovery channel on YouTube, Rory Irish posted a video (youtube.com/watch?v=P-6Rmhmmx-E&t=993s) where a Bronco Wildtrak slips off a rock with a sharp point that punctured the transmission pan. This is a difficult trail repair. While there is no external fluid-level dip stick, there is a plug on the side of the transmission for fluid replacement, and the plug has a dip stick internally. It's difficult to access and could be very difficult to fill the transmission with fluid on the trail. In addition, the plastic pan still needs repair. Aftermarket skid plates are available to protect the transmission pan.

The rear axle lower control arm forward mounts hang quite low and could easily be damaged. Adding skid plates to protect the mounts is a good idea.

are six changes that I would make before taking the Bronco off-road:

- Tie-rods: replace the stock, weak tie-rods with aftermarket units from Fabtech, Icon Vehicle Dynamics, or another aftermarket company.
- Steering-rack bushings: the bushing in the end of the steering rack can become displaced, leading to the pinion gear becoming disengaged from the rack teeth and causing a loss of steering. Replace the bushings with the kit from BroncBuster.
- Rocker panels: rock sliders (rocker slides) protect the rocker panels from expensive damage.
- Transmission pan: add a skid plate to protect the exposed plastic oil pan on the transmission.

- Goodyear Territory tires: upgrade the original equipment tires with off-road tires (all-terrain, rugged-terrain, or mud-terrain) from companies such as Falken, Mickey Thompson, Nexen, Nitto, or Hankook.
- Add a front sway-bar disconnect.

Replacing the vulnerable tie-rods should be the first upgrade on a new Bronco. In addition to the danger and difficult trail recovery, when the tie-rod breaks, it can cause the tie-rod end to pull out of the rack-and-pinion steering box, possibly damaging the CV joint at the outer end of the axle shaft.

The beadlock-capable wheels (part of the Sasquatch package) are attractive and durable, but the Goodyear Territory (Goodyear Wrangler on other non-Ford vehicles) tires leave a lot to be desired. I have tested more than 30 different off-road tires over the years. The OEM Goodyears offer the poorest performance of all of them. It's disappointing, but many great tire options are available.

The Goodyear Territory tires are actually the Goodyear Wrangler tire model rebranded for Ford, except the tire sidewall still reads "Wrangler Territory" in small type.

Conclusion

While some flaws in the Bronco Wildtrak created less-than-positive comments, in reality, some relatively minor upgrades to the Bronco make the Wildtrak model an excellent off-road machine, especially in desert terrain. The Bronco Wildtrak makes a comfortable and capable daily driver while being an excellent off-road vehicle.

Upgrade the steering (tie-rods and rack housing bushings) for safety, add a transmission skid plate and rock sliders for protection, and obtain better tires for performance. With those relatively minor upgrades, the Bronco Wildtrak can easily tackle 95 percent of the terrain in the US and even the most difficult street-legal trails with additional upgrades and an experienced driver. While axle articulation is limited (when compared to a solid-axle 4x4), careful line selection minimizes wheel lift and teeter-tottering.

The torque and horsepower of the 2.7L turbo V-6 EcoBoost engine makes the Bronco Wildtrak a great overlanding rig, especially for towing an off-road trailer. The Bronco's weight and capacity is good for overlanding, with a curb weight of 4,823 pounds, maximum towing capacity of 3,500 pounds, maximum payload of 1,196 pounds, and a gross weight of 6,020 pounds.

In spite of the concerns for safety, vehicle protection, and performance, I really like the Bronco Wildtrak two-door version. However, the four-door version is more practical for off-roading and for families, with increased storage and easier rear passenger seating (accessing the rear seat on the two-door is very difficult, even for small individuals). The biggest disappointment was the lack of grip from the Goodyear Territory MT tire. The negatives can be overcome easily. One member of the testing team liked the Bronco so much that he was ready to trade in his Nissan Frontier and take out a reverse mortgage on his house.

Front and rear lockers on the Bronco Wildtrak compensate for the poor traction offered by the Goodyear Territory mud-terrain tires.

Arguably, the 2.7L turbo V-6 EcoBoost engine in the Bronco Wildtrak is one of its best features. Great power allows quick acceleration and plenty of torque to take on steep hill climbs. Turbo lag is noticeable, but for rock crawling and slow trail sections, a little lack of power at low RPM means that engine torque will not kick in easily when making small throttle adjustments.

The Squeeze is a notorious trail located in the San Bernardino National Forest near Big Bear Lake, California. This narrow section requires precise driving to avoid vehicle damage. The Bronco Wildtrak is a wide vehicle that barely squeezes between the rocks. The Bronco Raptor would likely sustain damage here.

The Bronco Wildtrak is not quite as wide as my modified Jeep Wrangler, which is 6 inches wider than the stock Jeep Wrangler Rubicon.

TIRES AND WHEELS

Tire upgrades (specifically larger, taller tires) provide several advantages for Bronco owners: taller tires increase ground clearance and larger tires increase traction and add an aggressive appearance.

The most common questions that I receive from students and customers are: 1) "What tires do you run?" and 2) "What tires should I buy to upgrade my Bronco?" My answer to the second question is based on answers to the questions below:

- Will the Bronco be used as a daily driver or mostly as a trail rig?
- What type of terrain will you be traversing?
- In what conditions will you be driving (mud, snow, ice, sand, or rocks)?
- Will you be rock crawling?
- Will you be overlanding?
- Is noise an issue?
- Is tire wear an issue?
- Is the rig lifted? If so, how much?
- Are you using standard or bead-lock wheels?
- What size of tire do you prefer?
- What axles are being used?
- What is the axle gear ratio?

While many excellent all-terrain, mud-terrain, and hybrid tires are available, significant differences among tires can complicate the decision-making process. The problem relates to tire design and the effect of design and construction on performance—both on-road and off-road. Most tire store sales staff and technicians do not have the information in certain areas of design and construction to offer sound advice. Specifically, the areas of tread design and sidewall construction make a difference, but little information is available about the items.

The two common questions that were asked in the second paragraph are commonly posted on social media as well. Often, those who respond simply suggest the tire that they are using. Most people love their tires—and rightfully so. Tires require a big investment. Occasionally, people relay negative experiences. All of the information can be helpful, but the information is based on limited experience. Even those individuals

The Bronco Raptor features BFGoodrich KO2 all-terrain tires, which are far superior to the Goodyear Territory mud-terrain tires on some other Bronco models. (Photo Courtesy Ford Motor Company)

The BFGoodrich KO2 all-terrain tires on the Bronco Raptor are quiet and provide excellent handling on the highway. (Photo Courtesy Ford Motor Company)

The Goodyear Territory mud-terrain tires on the Wildtrak model are lacking off-road but seem to perform adequately in the snow. (Photo Courtesy Ford Motor Company)

The Bronco Everglades edition is equipped with the Goodyear Territory mud-terrain tires. Many other mud-terrain tires offer superior performance compared to the OEM tire. (Photo Courtesy Ford Motor Company)

LiteBright Nation's Kevin and Brittney Williams took their nearly stock Bronco Raptor on the Rubicon Trail. The biggest change was using the Nitto Trail Grappler mud-terrain tire to take on the nation's most notorious trail. (Photo Courtesy Kevin and Brittney Williams)

When the Trails 411 team tested the two-door Bronco Wildtrak, I was disappointed in the off-road performance of the OEM Goodyear Territory mud-terrain tire. I have tested about 30 different off-road tires over the last few years, and the Territory ranks last of all of the contemporary off-road tires.

Mud-terrain tires, such as the Falken WildPeak M/T tire (left), are generally preferred for serious off-road rigs. They are especially good on soft surfaces, where the large tread blocks and softer rubber compound increase grip. They also look more aggressive. All-terrain tires, such as the BFGoodrich TA all-terrain tire (middle), appeal to more casual off-road use due to better wear and a quieter ride on the highway. While the all-terrain tire may have a harder rubber compound, the increased tread area due to a smaller void ratio allows most all-terrain tires to perform with the equivalent mud-terrain tire in most off-road conditions. The Mickey Thompson Baja ATZ03 (right) all-terrain tire blurs the line between mud-terrain and all-terrain tires. More of a hybrid, the ATZ03 features large tread blocks, a smaller void ratio, numerous sipes in the tread blocks, and a rubber compound softer than a typical all-terrain tire but harder than a mud-terrain tire. Many tire companies have introduced this style of hybrid all-terrain tire. This new category is often called an "extreme all-terrain" tire or "rugged-terrain tire."

Tread patterns influence tire performance in many ways. On the road, the design of the tread blocks determines road noise. Off-road, the tread blocks affect performance on and in a variety of surfaces. For example, large tread blocks with big gaps between the blocks work well in soft surfaces, such as sand and wet mud. The big blocks can dig into the surface, acting somewhat like a paddle wheel. Smaller gaps between the blocks provide more surface area on the ground. This helps with traction on hard surfaces, such as the slick rock in Moab and on granite slabs like those found on the Rubicon Trail. All-terrain and hybrid tires work well on harder surfaces. Big tread blocks also flex more, which hurts steering feel slightly on the highway but helps the tires grip most surfaces better. The sipes (small slits cut into the tread blocks) can separate slightly under load, allowing improved grip. The lateral siping improves forward grip while braking or accelerating while the longitudinal sipes improve sideways grip. The longitudinal sipes help hold tires from sliding sideways on rocks and other higher-grip surfaces. The tire tread shown here depicts a wide range of tread design. Tread block sizes vary considerably (all-terrain tires versus mud-terrain tires), and the void ratios are also varying in size. Siping ranges from considerable to almost none. Most sipes are lateral with minimal longitudinal siping on most tread blocks.

who have used several brands and types of tires over a period of years offer input that is valid but lacks any direct comparisons.

Tire testing provides interesting insights into tire performance. Through the Trails 411 Off Road Training, tire comparison tests have been conducted for multiple tire companies. This testing experience has proven to be invaluable. In addition to being fun and challenging, considerable insight has been gained regarding the design parameters that affect off-road performance. While most tires are durable and well-designed, significant differences exist among the brands.

Off-Road Tires

The debate over mud-terrain versus all-terrain tires dates back to the creation of the first all-terrain tire in the 1970s. Now, the debate is more clouded with the advent of the hybrid tire, which is often called the rugged-terrain tire.

All-Terrain, Mud-Terrain, and Hybrid Tires

Hybrid tires fill the gap between mud-terrain tires and all-terrain tires. A hybrid off-road tire features more aggressive tread blocks and a larger void ratio compared to an all-terrain tire. The rubber compound is usually a little softer, so traction is better than a pure all-terrain tire, but wear is worse. While there has never been a clear winner in this argument, there are many factors to take into account, including highway miles versus off-road miles, weather conditions, terrain, the road surface, and noise. Two hybrid tires, including the Falken WildPeak A/T3W (released just a few years ago) and the Mickey Thompson Baja ATZ P3, have blurred the line that distinguishes all-terrain tires from mud-terrain tires even more.

Now, nearly every tire company that offers off-road tires markets these new-generation hybrid tires. They have more aggressive tread patterns and sidewalls than all-terrain tires while retaining a smaller void ratio for reduced noise on the highway and harder rubber compounds for better tire wear compared to a mud-terrain tire.

Hybrid off-road tires fall between the all-terrain and mud-terrain designs. The hybrid/rugged-terrain style of tire features larger tread blocks, larger void ratios, and a more aggressive look than an all-terrain tire but less so compared to an mud-terrain tire. From the left are the Falken Wildpeak AT3W, Nexen ATX, and Hankook XT. All of these tires perform exceptionally well off-road and are reasonably quiet on the road with good wear characteristics.

Mud-terrain tires offer the most aggressive look, using large tread blocks with a large void ratio and a softer rubber compound. They are noticeably louder on the road and wear more quickly due to the softer tread compound. Most mud-terrain tires work well in the rocks, but some designs lack good performance in the snow. From left to right are the Nitto Trail Grappler MT, Hankook MT2, Mickey Thompson Baja Boss MT, and Nexen Roadian MTX.

All-terrain tires feature smaller void ratios with more tread blocks, which are on the small side. From the left are the Nitto Ridge Grappler, Nexen AT, and BFGoodrich AT. Note the wide variety of tread designs and siping. The BFGoodrich is an older design. While the Nexen is the least aggressive design, it performs quite well off-road. The Nitto is more aggressive and somewhat louder. In general, all-terrain tires are quieter, wear longer, and are the least-aggressive style of off-road tire.

Ply Ratings, Tire Cutting, and Slashing

Cutting or puncturing a tire tread or slashing a sidewall occurs off-road and is somewhat rare due to modern tire design and technology. Areas with sharp rocks are the most likely to cause problems. Two factors reduce the possibility of serious tire damage: 1) run only load ranges D, E, or F tires and 2) lower the tire pressure (as described later in this chapter.)

The load range refers to the ply rating. Old bias-ply tires had a ply rating of up to 10 ply for light truck and off-road tires. With modern materials, fewer plies are needed to achieve the same strength and puncture resistance. A radial tire with a D rating is equivalent to an 8-ply bias-ply tire, an E rating is equivalent to a 10-ply bias-ply tire, and an F rating is equivalent to a 12-ply bias-ply tire. Tires with these ratings provide the best protection off-road. Note that the load rating does not reflect the stiffness of the sidewall. Sidewall stiffness relates mostly to sidewall construction, especially the angle of the sidewall cords.

Tread Design Differences

The most obvious difference among the all-terrain, hybrid, and mud-terrain tire is in the tread design. A mud-terrain tire features more-aggressive tread blocks and a larger void ratio. The void ratio is the percentage of the total tread block area versus the area of the total tire tread. The tread blocks on a mud-terrain tire tend to be larger and thicker than an all-terrain tire, and the blocks on a hybrid are somewhere in between. The thin slits in the tread (sipes) allow the tread to flex and the edges to better grip on hard surfaces, such as rocks. Sipes are used in all-terrain, hybrid, and mud-terrain tires. Generally, an all-terrain tire has more sipes. This improves its grip on hard surfaces. The new, more-aggressive hybrid tires create as much (or possibly slightly more) grip

The void ratio of a tire tread measures the area of tread blocks versus the area of the gaps between the tread blocks (white in the illustration). All-terrain tires use a small void ratio, meaning that more rubber is on the ground. Mud-terrain tires use much larger void ratios, meaning that less rubber is on the ground but there is more ability for the tire to grip a surface, especially soft surfaces like mud, sand, and snow. Larger void ratios also create more noise on the highway.

Load capacity refers to the load-carrying capabilities of a tire. Most off-road tires have a fairly high load-carrying capacity. Load capacity requires careful consideration for overlanding vehicles. Heavily loaded Broncos full of overlanding gear need higher load-capacity tires. For example, the Mickey Thompson Baja Boss A/T in the 33X11.50R17LT size has a load range E (10 ply equivalent) and load capacity of 3,195 pounds at 80 psi, which is very high. The total load capacity of this tire would be over 12,000 pounds at 80 psi. The load capacity will drop considerably as tire pressures are reduced. The same tire in the 33X12.50R17LT size has a load range D rating (8 ply) with a load capacity of 2,600 pounds at 50 psi.

than the same-size mud-terrain tire.

While a good mud-terrain tread design can keep rocks from lodging between tread blocks, the design must also eject mud and snow. Some designs do this more efficiently than others. In general, the larger void ratio of a mud-terrain tire is better in soft surface conditions, but the tread blocks need to flex to eject snow and dense mud. Tread design plays a role, but so does tire pressure. Lower tire pressure helps when the voids become filled with debris, ice, snow, or heavy mud. Some all-terrain tread designs are better in snow but lacking in the ability to keep small stones out of the tread voids.

Sidewall Design

One of the most important elements of tire design is the structure of the sidewall. When four-wheeling on rocks, in ruts, or on side slopes, it is critical for the sidewall tread to have good grip. A lack of grip means

that the tire can slide sideways off the edge of a rock, the slope on a side hill, or within a series of ruts. Slipping can alter your desired path. If you slip, you might bang a rock slider, skid plate, or bumper on a rock that you thought you could avoid. The tire sidewall needs to flex to conform to the road surface and to have a design that allows rocks and snow to be ejected from the tread pattern. Most off-road tires do a better job of keeping tread voids cleared when aired down to a lower pressure.

Void Ratio and Tread Blocks

The void ratio of a tire indicates how much of the surface of the tire tread is covered with tread blocks versus the area void of rubber. Higher void ratios result in less traction on hard surfaces but usually more traction on soft surfaces because the tread block digs into the surface. Tread-block design affects traction and road noise. Taller tread blocks

work better in soft surfaces, such as sand, mud, and especially soft silt. Tires with smaller void ratios have more surface area on the ground but usually use a harder rubber compound.

Tire Diameter and Ground Clearance

One major reason to upgrade to larger tires is to gain ground clearance. Just as important is the ability to run at lower tire pressures. Closely related to tire diameter is the diameter of the wheel. The smaller the wheel, the larger the tire sidewall will be. The smallest wheel that is practical on a Bronco is 17 inches in diameter. A large-diameter wheel will reduce the sidewall height and reduce the capacity for lower tire pressures. A 17-inch-diameter wheel is highly desirable for any size of tire—even a 40-inch-diameter monster. At a 17-inch diameter, tire pressures can be optimized for more traction and improved ride quality.

Driving side slopes, ruts and rocks often create a situation where the sidewall will come in contact with the surface. Sidewall traction becomes very important in these situations. Often, the sidewall is the only portion of the tire touching the ground. Aggressive sidewall designs aid sidewall grip.

The Bronco Wildtrak with 35-inch-tall tires clears the hump easily. A smaller tire may allow contact with the ground. Without rock sliders protecting the rocker panels, this can cause damage. Taller tires increase ground clearance.

Off-Road

Off-road, the advantages of the all-terrain versus mud-terrain tires is less clear. In some conditions, the mud-terrain tire provides a slight advantage, but the differences are minor. The biggest factor is the type of surface. Most hybrid tires outperform all-terrain tires and challenge the mud-terrain tires for traction supremacy.

Hard Surfaces

For the most part, the all-terrain tire is better on hard surfaces. While the rubber compound is a little harder, the void ratio is smaller, meaning that more rubber is on the ground for equal-size tires at similar pressures. The advantage diminishes when the surfaces are wet. The hybrid tires that were recently tested seem to outperform the all-terrain tires and may offer better grip on hard-rock and slick-rock terrain when compared to an mud-terrain tire. A lower void ratio than a mud-terrain tire and a slightly softer tread compound

Rubber Compound and Wear

All-terrain tires tend to have harder rubber compounds than mud-terrain tires (the hybrid is in between), so the mud-terrain tire will wear more quickly (with all else being equal). Even though the all-terrain tire is harder, it has more rubber on the road or trail surface due to a smaller void ratio. This usually means that the all-terrain tire will have slightly better traction on hard surfaces (given equal tire sizes). The mud-terrain will grip better on soft surfaces. This is best witnessed when the tire is operating *in* a surface (as opposed to *on* a surface), such as in sand; mud; snow; and soft, loose dirt (as opposed to asphalt; ice; or hard, packed dirt). The hybrid tire offers the best of both worlds with excellent performance on hard surfaces.

A durometer tests rubber hardness. Higher numbers indicate harder rubber compounds. A hardness number in the 60 range is relatively soft for an off-road tire.

Hard surfaces generally offer good grip if dry and not covered in dust or sand. In some cases, the tire sidewall grip comes in play to keep the tire from sliding off a rock or dirt slope.

than an all-terrain tire provides a noticeable advantage.

Soft Surfaces

Due to deeper, larger tread blocks, the mud-terrain tire performs at its best in soft surfaces. Mud, sand, loose dirt, and snow are conditions in which the mud-terrain tire provides the best performance. In certain types of snow (especially in slushy, sticky snow conditions), the mud-terrain tire has an advantage only if the tread design and lower tire pressures are able to eject the snow from the tread voids. The hybrid tread pattern works well on slippery surfaces.

Rock crawling places a premium on tire traction. Tire sidewalls are often the only part of a tire in contact with the rock. The sidewall tread pattern design affects traction.

Tire Size and Off-Road Performance

Tires with a larger diameter and wider tread width have a larger rubber contact patch on the ground, especially with low tire pressures. This improves traction. Since taller tire sidewalls can tolerate lower tire pressures with a greater reduction in sidewall height, the ride quality is better. The downside of larger tires is increased brake and steering system wear. Fuel economy also takes a negative hit.

Large-diameter wheels, such as the 20-inch wheel here, reduce the tire's sidewall height. Smaller sidewalls translate into less opportunity to lower tire pressures for improved traction and ride comfort.

In some cases, many believe that a taller but narrower tire works better in deep mud surfaces. This is true to a point. If the narrower tire can penetrate the mud down to the harder surface below the mud, then traction may be slightly better. However, in nearly all cases, a wider tire offers superior traction.

Siping

Sipes are thin cuts in the tread of a tire. They allow the tire tread to separate slightly, which improves traction on ice and snow. For off-road

Lateral sipes across the tread help increase forward traction, which improves acceleration and braking performance on dirt and rocks.

use, siping can improve traction when rock crawling. Depending on the siping pattern, it can also increase lateral grip, helping to hold the tire sideways on rocks, side slopes, and ruts.

Lateral Grooves and Crosscuts

Lateral grooves and crosscuts are similar to siping but larger. This allows tread blocks to flex and grip

Longitudinal and angled sipes will separate slightly under load, helping to increase traction laterally to the sides. This helps hold the tire on side slopes and slanted rocks.

soft surfaces and uneven terrain more effectively. At lower tire pressures, grooves and crosscuts can flex to help expel small stones, snow, and mud from the tread voids for better traction.

Forward and Side Grip

Tread and sidewall design play a major role in how a tire grips in low-traction situations. Good forward traction is critical for climbing and descending large rocks and hills. Side traction is crucial for holding onto side slopes, ruts, bumps, and rocks. Tire designs are a compromise. Various designs are better in certain off-road situations.

Tire Pressure

The first reason to reduce tire pressure (air down the tires) is to increase the tire's contact patch (footprint), which increases traction.

Second, it improves ride comfort on rough terrain. It is impossible to use soft-enough springs to make the ride comfortable. Since a tire sidewall is essentially a spring, lower tire pressures improve ride comfort. While lower tire pressures improve ride comfort for the passengers, they also reduce the loading on the chassis, suspension, and driveline in rough terrain. This reduces wear on critical components.

Third, the lower tire pressures allow the tire to conform to rocks, ruts, bumps, and other obstacles. This improves traction.

Fourth, it reduces the probability of a tire puncture. When a tire is at lower pressures, it is more compliant and better resists a puncture from rocks and sharp objects.

Finally, lower tire pressures reduce damage to the road surface.

Without reduced tire pressure, the Bronco Wildtrak would experience excessive wheelspin, resulting in a diagonal climb.

Reduced tire pressures improve ride quality over rough terrain and help keep the tires stay planted to the ground.

High tire pressures affect the ability of the tire to wrap around rocks. When a tire can conform to the shape of a rock, traction improves significantly. The Nexen Roadian MTX mud-terrain tire has a flexible sidewall compared to some other tires. The tire pressure shown here would vary for different tires. Most tires would need a lower pressure to obtain the same amount of tire flex and conformity.

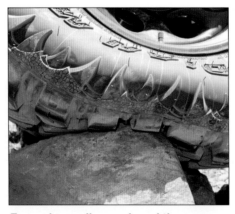

For rock crawling, reduced tire pressures allow the tire tread to wrap around the rock, greatly increasing traction and reducing the possibility of a puncture on a sharp, pointed rock.

Tire grip on the side of a sloped rock can make the difference between clearing an obstacle and sliding off the rock. Sliding off the rock can cause the vehicle to become stuck and cause possible damage to rocker panels or other exposed body sections.

Studies have determined that running at lower pressures spreads the load on the tire over a greater area (larger tire contact patch), and this actually reduces damage to the road surface. Less damage translates into less erosion.

As a side note, I have observed (but not tested) that different tires on the same vehicle on the same stretch of road will generate different amounts of dust. Different tire pressures on the same tire have the same effect. Lower pressures make less dust. The only downside to airing down is reduced ground clearance. One trick that I use if I get high-centered on an obstacle and do not have enough traction to move forward or backward is to air up one or more of the tires to gain a little more ground clearance.

Optimal Off-Road Tire Pressure Range

Every off-road tire and vehicle combination has an optimal tire-pressure range for off-road driv-

ing. The goal when setting the tire pressure for going off-road is to maximize the size of the tire contact patch without lowering the tire pressure so much that tire damage is likely on rough surfaces. Two factors contribute to the optimal tire pressure: 1) sidewall stiffness and 2) vehicle weight on the tire.

More flexible tire sidewalls need more pressure at the optimal setting. Heavier vehicles need higher pressure at the optimal pressure. A simple measurement allows you to determine the optimal pressure on your Bronco. I learned this procedure several years ago from Harry Llewellyn of Coyote Enterprises (Coyote Deflators) and have used it on many tires ever since.

The goal is to find a pressure that expands the tire contact patch on the ground (squishes the tire) without lowering the pressure so low that the tire bead can come unseated or the bead and sidewall can be damaged if it becomes pinched between the wheel's rim and a rock (or the ground). Llewellyn determined that the sidewall height from the ground to the bottom of the rim was important. He also determined that reducing pressure in the tire from fully inflated to a measurement of between 75 and 90 percent of maximum pressure meets the criteria for the optimal tire contact patch and protecting the tire from damage. For relatively smooth roads, the 90-percent height works well. For most off-roading in dry conditions, 85 percent is just about perfect. For soft surfaces, such as sand, mud, or snow, between 75 and 80 percent works well.

When I began measuring sidewalls, I would inflate to the maximum inflation pressure listed on the tire sidewall. I quickly learned

that there is virtually no difference between maximum inflation pressure (up to 80 psi on some tires) and an inflation pressure of about 40 to 50 psi. I use 40 psi as a starting point and measure the tire sidewall height from the ground to the bottom of the wheel's rim.

For most off-road situations, I deflate the tire until the measurement is 85 percent of the maximum inflation pressure (40 to 50 psi). For sand or snow, I'll drop down to around 75 percent or slightly taller. For example, a 37-inch tire on a 17-inch-diameter rim will have a fully inflated sidewall height of 10 inches (in reality, no 37-inch-diameter tire is actually 37 inches tall). Deflate the tire to the 85-percent height, as 85 percent of 10 inches is 8.5 inches. Take note of the pressure, as this pressure is your optimal pressure for normal rock-crawling and off-road situations. Use the same tire pressure gauge at all times for consistency. Tire pressure gauges vary considerably in accuracy.

If you are overlanding and add weight to your Bronco for a trip, make sure to adjust the tire pressure to compensate for the additional load. A heavy load may require up to 5 psi higher tire pressures for off-road driving.

Every tire responds differently to inflation pressures. To put the difference between tire brands into perspective, I have seen as much as a 6-psi variance from a soft-sidewall tire to a very-stiff-sidewall tire on the same corner of the same vehicle. One tire may be at optimal pressure at 15 psi, which means that beadlock rims are not necessary, while another tire on the same rig may need only 9 psi for the optimal pressure. Any pressure below 10 or 11 psi should be using beadlock wheels for safety. Another factor to consider is a new tire versus an older one that has been used for several hundred miles. Once a tire is broken in, recheck the sidewall measurements. The tire will become more flexible after driving off-road at lower tire pressures. I have seen as much as a 3-psi pressure increase to get back to the optimal sidewall height pressure after a single day of off-roading.

The Falken Wildpeak MT01 features a stiff sidewall construction. This tire needs to be aired down more to achieve the same tire contact spread as a softer-sidewall tire. At the top, the tire pressure is 28 psi. In the middle, the pressure is about 12 psi, which is about the lowest advisable for non-beadlock wheels. The bottom tire is aired down to 6 psi. The tire conforms to the rock much more effectively. This series of photos was taken on a heavier vehicle. A lighter vehicle would need even lower tire pressures for contact patch compliance.

The BFGoodrich TA KO2 all-terrain tire (top left) has one of the more aggressive sidewall designs. The siping allows flex for better grip. The ridges between the sidewall tread blocks are stepped to help eject rocks and debris from the sidewall. The Mickey Thompson Baja ATZ P3 all-terrain tire (top right) has a sidewall design more like a mud-terrain tire. This sidewall design grips very well on rock edges and the sides of ruts where little or no tread is gripping the surface. The Falken WildPeak AT03 (bottom left) has an aggressive sidewall for an all-terrain tire. The stepped ridges on the upper part of the sidewall progressively grip the edges of rocks and slopes for better grip. They also dig into soft surfaces for even more bite. The Nexen Roadian AT all-terrain tire (bottom right) has a conservative sidewall design, but the triangular shaped scallops on the lower portion of the sidewall provide a surprising amount of grip on loose dirt and large, sloped rocks.

One factor affecting tire traction relates to tire pressure. The Nexen Roadian MTX mud-terrain tire features a fairly flexible sidewall construction. These tire contact patch impressions show the actual tire contact patch area at four different inflation settings. Little difference exists between contact patch areas at 50 psi versus 27 psi. Major increases exist in contact patch area at 14 and 10 psi. The larger the contact patch area, the greater the increase in traction. The contact patch increases by more than double when airing down from 27 psi to 14 psi. From 27 psi to 10 psi, the contact patch area nearly triples.

35 PSI

26 PSI

18 PSI

14 PSI

10 PSI

Tire pressures affect the ability of the tire to wrap around rocks. When a tire can conform to the shape of a rock, traction improves significantly. The Nexen Roadian MTX mud-terrain tire has a flexible sidewall compared to some other tires. The tire pressure shown here would vary for different tires. Most tires would need a lower pressure to obtain the same amount of tire flex and conformity.

Sidewall Bulge

Tire pressures indicate an arbitrary measurement. The tire sidewall height (or bulge in the sidewall) provides the ultimate measure of how well the tire will perform off-road. The sidewall height can be easily measured, as can the bulge in the sidewall.

Looking straight down at the tire sidewall from above, you can see the bulge. Place a carpenter's square on

The Toyo Tires Open Country RT Trail features large tread blocks with siping and a low void ratio, which keeps noise to a minimum. The large sidewall lugs protect the tire sidewall while offering great traction from the sidewall in side-slope and steeply slanted rock situations.

The Toyo Tires Open Country RT Trail wraps around rocks, providing good traction for rock crawling. Tire pressure here is 15 psi.

the ground against the tire's sidewall at normal inflation. Then, put a mark on the road where the square rests. Deflate the tire to the optimal tire pressure and place the square against the tire sidewall. Make a second mark and measure the bulge. This is a second measurement and provides an excellent visual reference point.

The longitudinal siping on the Nexen Roadian MTX tire improves lateral grip, helping the tire stay on the sloped rock.

Tire Compliance over Rocks and Obstacles

Often overlooked as an important tire characteristic is the ability of a tire to wrap around rocks and other obstacles. Airing down to optimal tire pressures allows this. Tire compliance is important when climbing up large rocks. Undercut ledges can be very difficult to climb if the ledge is taller than the centerline of the wheel. For example, the ledge might be 24 inches tall, and the Bronco might have a 37-inch tire. The lip of the ledge is above the center of the tire, which means that the tire must move backward to climb forward. The only way that this can happen is if the tire has a low enough tire pressure to conform to the rock. As the tire wraps around the rock, the tire compresses and allows the Bronco to

When the tire sidewall flexes enough to wrap around a rock, traction is significantly increased and there is less chance of a puncture. Here, the Nexen Roadian MTX is aired down to 14 psi. The sidewall is relatively soft. This F-rated tire is more flexible than most D-rated sidewalls. The sidewall rating does not determine the sidewall stiffness. The angle of the cords in the sidewall plays a major role in sidewall stiffness.

Many screw-on tire deflators are on the market. The Coyote deflators provide the most consistent air-down pressures and are very reliable. Many screw-on deflators require readjustment after a few uses. The Coyote deflators come with a lifetime warranty.

The RockJock deflator removes the valve core from the valve stem on the wheel. This allows rapid deflation to the desired tire pressure. To use the RockJock deflator, screw the fitting onto the valve stem, depress the plunger, rotate until it captures the valve core, unscrew the valve core, pull the plunger out, open the air valve to deflate, and close the air valve to check pressure. When the desired pressure is reached, keep the valve closed, push in the plunger, screw in the valve core until it is snug, and pull the plunger out so that the valve core cannot be unscrewed while unscrewing the fitting from the valve stem. Unscrew the fitting from the valve stem and replace the valve cap.

climb the rock face. If the tire pressure is too high, the tire will not compress enough and the tire will try to push the whole vehicle backward, which makes forward progress very difficult (or impossible).

Tire Deflator Types

Using tire deflators is the easiest way to air down tires when you hit the trails. In general, there are three types of deflators. Many tire pressure gauges have a release valve for releasing air from a tire. These are very slow and require constant attention. Second, there are deflators that screw onto the valve stem and depress the spring-loaded valve core. These are adjustable for minimum pressure when they automatically shut off. They usually come in sets of two or four. Not much faster than a pressure gauge but with four and automatic shut off, you can screw them on and walk away. The third deflator also screws onto the valve stem, but it unscrews the valve core from the stem while capturing it within the nozzle. They have a pres-

The Apex Performance Rapid Precision valve allows speedy tire deflation and inflation. The Rapid Precision valve replaces the standard valve stem and core. The deflator uses a sliding lever to open ports in the body, allowing extremely fast airing down. A 40-inch-diameter tire can be aired down from 30 psi to 9 psi in about 20 seconds. All four tires can be aired down before four screw-on deflators can be attached. Be aware that it is easy to air down too much. Attention is needed. (Photo Courtesy Apex Performance)

sure gauge and on-off pressure relief valve for accurate control of tire pressure. This allows for very rapid airing down. One of these deflators is typically faster than four of the others. A downside is the need to watch the pressure as it drops.

One style of system for airing up and down uses four hoses and a manifold to provide air to all four tires at once. These systems work with compressors or with a Power Tank. This adds to the ease and speed of altering tire pressures and has the added advantage of equalizing the pressure in all four tires. Several companies offer this type of system, including SpeedFlate, MorrFlate, and FasterFlate.

Power Tank offers Monster Valves, which require an additional hole in the wheel for a larger valve stem. A gauge is used on the normal valve stem to monitor pressure, while the larger valve releases pressure very quickly. A similar product is the Apex Performance Deflator. This product replaces the standard valve stems with a new valve with a sliding lever that opens ports to rapidly release pressure. A pressure gauge is on the stem to monitor the pressure. The valve lever is closed when the desired pressure is achieved.

Reinflating Tires

Reinflating tires before hitting the asphalt reduces the risk of a tire failure. A tire with low pressure will easily overheat as the distance and the speed increases. Ambient air tem-

perature is also a factor. Driving short distances at lower speeds on days when the temperature is moderate is acceptable. However, reinflating tires back to normal highway pressure is important. There are two ways to air up the tires: using a compressor or using a CO_2 tank.

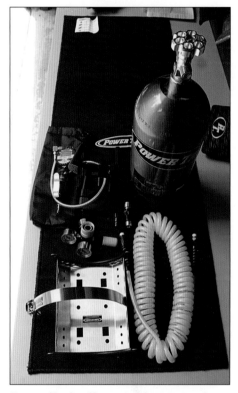

Power Tank offers a wide range of CO_2 tanks, regulators, mounts, hoses, gauges, and accessories. The Power Tank is the fastest way to air up tires. It uses compressed CO_2 to inflate tires or drive air tools. I air up all four 37-inch tires from 14 psi to 30 psi in about 3 minutes, including moving from tire to tire. This compares to about 20 minutes with an onboard air compressor. The Power Tank is also quieter and more reliable than an electric air compressor. The downside is the need to refill the tank with CO_2. CO_2 is available from paintball shops, some welding supply shops, and beverage-dispensing equipment stores.

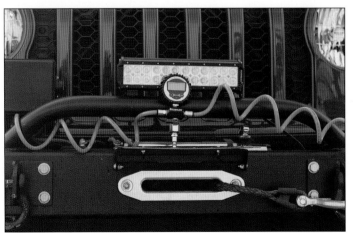

The Speedflate airing system uses four hoses attached to manifolds so that all four tires can be aired up or down simultaneously.

ARB offers a dual compressor system allowing tires to be aired up quickly. Air axle lockers are easily operated. Air tools can also be used with the ARB dual compressors.

Viair makes a range of portable air compressors in a variety of outputs and duty cycles.

Onboard compressors are best. Portable compressors are less expensive but are slow and overheat easily. Pay attention to the duty cycle. A duty cycle refers to how frequently an air compressor can be run over a certain period of time. For example, if an air compressor has a 100-percent duty cycle, that means it can run continuously without needing to rest and cool down. Air compressors with a 75-percent duty cycle will run for three-fourths of the total cycle time. In other words, if a compressor has a 60-second cycle time, it will run pressurized air for 45 seconds of each minute. Most standard compressors have a duty cycle between 50 and 100 percent. Do not run compressors too long because dam-

age can result. Onboard compressors are convenient but operate slowly and are noisy.

The second option is to use a CO_2 tank, such as the Power Tank. A Power Tank is the fastest way to inflate tires. The Power Tank Monster Valve allows even faster airing up (and down as well). The downside to a Power Tank is the need to have them refilled with CO_2. The speed and convenience of airing up at the end of a day on the trail has made the Power Tank a popular airing-up option.

Sidewall Height Reduction

The chart below is a quick-reference guide to determine the optimal amount that the tire sidewall should be reduced for the ideal tire contact patch spread and tire sidewall squash. These measurements are approximate but will be close. Use 10 percent for fairly smooth roads where speeds are higher. I use 12.5 percent for most off-road situations and 15 percent to 25 percent for soft surfaces and low speeds.

Wheel Diameter	Tire Diameter	Sidewall Height Reduction Range		
		10 Percent	12.5 Percent	15 Percent
15	32	0.85	1.06	1.28
15	33	0.90	1.13	1.35
15	35	1.00	1.25	1.50
15	37	1.10	1.38	1.65
16	32	0.80	1.00	1.20
16	33	0.85	1.06	1.28
16	35	0.95	1.19	1.43
17	32	0.75	0.94	1.13
17	33	0.80	1.00	1.20
17	35	0.90	1.13	1.35
17	37	1.00	1.25	1.50
17	40	1.15	1.44	1.73
17	42	1.25	1.56	1.88
20	32	0.60	0.75	0.90
20	33	0.65	0.81	0.98
20	35	0.75	0.94	1.13
20	37	0.85	1.06	1.28
20	40	1.00	1.25	1.50
20	42	1.10	1.38	1.65

Note: All measurements are in inches.

Measuring Tire Heights

To optimize aired-down tire pressures, the tire dimensions are critical. In the "Tire Pressure" section in this chapter, the formula for airing down requires a measurement of the tire sidewall from the bottom of the rim (or beadlock ring) to the ground at full inflation. The pressure is reduced to 85 percent to 90 percent of that measurement for general off-road driving and most rock-crawling situations. For soft surfaces, such as mud, deep snow, and especially sand, the tire pressure can be reduced to about 75 percent (85 percent of the full-inflation sidewall height).

Inflate the tire to the maximum pressure noted on the tire's sidewall or to about 40 to 50 psi (whichever is less). Tire sidewall heights change very little above 40 psi.

Measure the distance from the ground to the bottom of the wheel rim. Note that the bottom of the rim is about 1/4 inch lower than the bead of the tire. A tire for a 17-inch wheel will measure close to 17 inches from tire bead to tire bead (diameter), so measuring to the bottom of the wheel rim will be about a 1/4 inch less. I use 85 to 90 percent of this measurement as a guide for off-road tire pressures. If the sidewall is very short, use 90 percent or less (for example, a 32-inch tire on a 20-inch rim can be aired down very little). When driving in conditions with sand, mud, or deep snow, use 80 percent.

Multiply the measurement in Step 2 by 0.90 (or the amount that you feel is correct for your situation). Install a deflator.

Here is an example using a 35-inch tire on a 17-inch wheel: The distance from the ground to the bottom of the wheel rim will be about 8.75 inches. It is less than 9 inches because the tire is not actually 35 inches in diameter (it is slightly smaller). In addition, the measurement is taken at the bottom of the rim and not the tire bead, which is covered by the wheel rim.

Reduce the tire pressure to the new ideal sidewall height. The 85- to 90-percent measurement works in most cases off-road. The goal is to keep the tire sidewall from becoming pinched between the wheel rim and a hard surface or rock. Be sure to reinflate the tires to normal highway pressures when you reach the highway.

Measure the tire pressure with a good, consistent tire-pressure gauge.

For soft surfaces, such as sand, mud, and snow, reduce the pressure even more. You can go as low as the 75-percent number for sand and deep snow.

The same drop in sidewall height can be used on all four tires.

Always use the same tire-pressure gauge. I tested several pressure gauges compared to a calibrated, highly accurate gauge. The variation is up to 4 psi on the same tire at 15 psi— that's over 25-percent variation, which is huge. The actual pressure number is irrelevant as long as the same gauge is used every time. ■

Step 1: Inflate the tire to the maximum pressure noted on the tire sidewall or to about 50 psi, whichever is less. Tire sidewall heights change very little above 50 psi.

Step 2: Measure the distance from the ground to the bottom of the wheel rim. I use 85 percent of this measurement as a guide for off-road tire pressures. If the sidewall is very short, use 90 percent. In some cases, such as terrain with sand, mud, and deep snow, use 80 percent.

Step 3: Multiply the measurement in Step 2 by 0.85 (or the amount you feel is correct for your situation). Install a deflator. Here's an example using a 35-inch-tall tire on a 17-inch wheel: The ground to the bottom of the wheel rim will be about 8.5 inches. It is less than 9.0 inches because the tire is not actually 35 inches in diameter but slightly smaller. In addition, the measurement is taken at the bottom of the rim, not the top of the tire sidewall.

Step 4: Reduce the tire pressure to the new ideal sidewall height. The 85-percent measurement works in most cases off-road. The goal is to keep the tire sidewall from becoming pinched between the wheel rim and a hard surface or rock. Be sure to reinflate the tires to normal highway pressures.

Wheels

Most Bronco models come equipped with wheels with good off-road capability. The Badlands, Sasquatch package–equipped Broncos, Wildtrak, and Everglades models use either 8- or 8.5-inch-wide wheels that are ideal for upgrading to more capable and taller tires. The base model has 16-inch-diameter wheels. The Outer Banks version comes on 18-inch wheels, while all other models use 17-inch-diameter wheels. The models with the available Sasquatch package feature beadlock-capable wheels. Beadlock-capable wheels can be used as traditional wheels with a beauty ring with standard mounting, or they can use a beadlock ring (an extra-cost option) to mount tires, as beadlocks allow lower tire pressures to be utilized and reduce the risk of the tire becoming unseated from the wheel rim.

Many aftermarket companies offer a wide range of wheels in a variety of styles for the Bronco in the

Stock Bronco Wheel Specifications				
Model	Wheel Size	Wheel Offset	Bolt Pattern	Wheel Backspacing
Base	16x7	+55 mm	6x139.7	5.7 inches
Big Bend	17x7.5	+55 mm	6x139.7	5.9 inches
Outer Banks	18x7.5	+55 mm	6x139.7	5.9 inches
Black Diamond	17x7.5	+55 mm	6x139.7	5.9 inches
Badlands	17x8	+55 mm	6x139.7	5.9 inches
Sasquatch, Wildtrak, Everglades, 1st Edition, Heritage	17x8.5	+30 mm	6x139.7	5.4 inches
Bronco Raptor	17x8	+55 mm	6x139.7	6.2 inches

stock 6 on 139.7-mm wheel lug pattern. Most aftermarket Bronco wheels are from 8 to 9 inches wide. Be aware that stock Bronco wheels use a large backspace to minimize track width. Be sure that the backspacing on aftermarket wheels is greater on a wider wheel and with a wider tire to assure adequate tire clearance when turning full lock, especially on rutted and bumpy terrain.

Aftermarket wheel selections for Broncos are available in the hundreds. When upgrading wheels, several choices must be made. Items requiring consideration include aluminum alloy versus steel, wheel diameter and width, backspacing, standard versus beadlock designs, tire size, tire clearance, and valve-stem vulnerability. Lug bolt hole configurations come into play only if axle bolt patterns are changed from stock.

Alloy versus Steel

The two materials used in the manufacturing of wheels offer different advantages. Steel is less expensive, and it is strong and malleable. This means the wheel will bend on impact but not crack or break. A bent steel wheel can be hammered back (though with great difficulty) into a reasonable shape to hold air if deformed on the trail. A cracked

or broken alloy wheel cannot be repaired. Any wheel can be (and probably will be) scratched, gouged, or more severely damaged when off-roading, especially on the more extreme rock-crawling trails.

An extensive range of styles is available for alloy wheels, and they are lighter than steel (for the same size). In addition, aluminum alloys dissipate heat better than steel, helping to cool the brakes under extreme conditions. Costs vary considerably with alloy wheels.

The OEM wheel on the Bronco Wildtrak features a beadlock-capable design. The outer ring is a beauty ring. When removed, the ring allows the tire mounting to be reconfigured for a beadlock setup when the optional beadlock rings are purchased.

Steel wheels are standard on the base Bronco and Black Diamond editions. Steel wheels absorb heavy impacts better than alloy wheels. The steel wheel is less expensive but weighs more than the alloy counterparts.

Alloy wheels weigh less than steel wheels but cost substantially more. Raceline makes a wide range of off-road alloy wheels with and without simulated beadlock styling.

Beadlock-capable wheels are standard with the Sasquatch package (which is standard on the Wildtrak). The beadlock rings are sold separately. The Bronco Raptor is equipped with the beadlock rings.

Raceline makes bulletproof beadlock wheels available in standard alloy versions as well as forged (very expensive) models. It also makes steel beadlock wheels.

Alloy wheel manufacturing uses four different processes: forging, high-pressure die-casting, low-pressure die-casting, and gravity casting. Forged wheels are the toughest and strongest but also much more expensive. Many forged wheels are not street legal and are mostly used for competition.

Cast wheels are by far the most common. The casting process is less important than the quality of the materials used in the process. Although they are rare, cast wheels can crack or even break from hard off-road impacts.

Standard Bead versus Beadlocks

Close manufacturing tolerances for current wheels and tires allow a tight fitment between the wheel bead and the tire bead. For this reason, most Bronco owners can use a standard-bead wheel (like the stock wheels). Beadlock-style wheels look like beadlocks wheels but have a standard wheel bead. A true beadlock wheel has an outer ring that bolts to the wheel. The beadlock ring holds the tire bead in place so

The beauty rings on the beadlock-capable wheels, which are standard on the Wildtrak and the Sasquatch package, can be removed without deflating the tires for maintenance or repainting.

that it cannot become dislodged from the wheel at low pressures in extreme conditions. Some Bronco models feature beadlock-capable wheels, allowing tires to be mounted as traditional-bead wheels or as beadlocks with the optional beadlock ring.

I have tested many different tire pressures for soft surface, low-speed four-wheeling. This is usually a low enough pressure for adequate traction. A rule of thumb for tire pressures on a standard, non-beadlock rim is a minimum of 10 psi. More extreme situations, such as deep

Icon Vehicle Dynamics offers a complete line of alloy wheels for off-road use. The Alpha wheel on the left is a 6-lug design for the Bronco and features a bronze matte finish with a satin black ring. The wheel size is 17x8.5 inches. On the right is the Icon Vehicle Dynamics Rebound Pro wheel 6 lug with matte bronze finish.

snow, wet, muddy, or snow-covered rocks, require lower pressures, as do tires with a very stiff sidewall. This is where beadlocks are necessary. Beadlocks have been tested at tire pressures as low as 3 psi in the snow and on soft surfaces, such as sand and mud, and on snowy, muddy rocks on black diamond trails.

Icon Vehicle Dynamics's newest innovation in beadlock wheels is the Recon-Pro with a 17-inch diameter. They are available in the Bronco 6-lug bolt pattern.

The Icon Vehicle Dynamics Recon Pro features the company's patented Inner-Lock Department of Transportation (DOT)–compliant bead-retention technology with aggressive 16-spoke styling. The Recon PRO was initially available in the 17x8.5-inch size for 6-lug applications for the Bronco. InnerLock Technology uses a series of high-strength alloy bead-retention pins inserted through a thickened section of the wheel to act as a fence to physically prevent the tire bead from being pushed away from the wheel's inner lip.

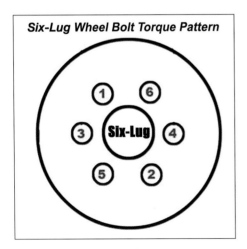

Six-Lug Wheel Bolt Torque Pattern

Torquing wheel lug nuts to the proper torque and in the correct sequence is important. The torque bolt-pattern chart shows the correct lug-torquing sequence for 6-lug Bronco wheels.

three stages on Raceline beadlock wheels, starting with 12 ft-lbs, progressing to 14 ft-lbs, and ending at 16 ft-lbs. Then, I double-check the torque of all bolts. Different wheel manufacturers may have different torque specifications. You must also check torque settings monthly to assure reliability and safety. All bolts should be replaced annually.

Diameter

Most stock wheels on the Bronco are 17-inches in diameter, except on the base model and Outer Banks model. The ideal wheel diameter for the Bronco is 17 inches, which is the smallest possible wheel diameter that fits most models. A larger-diameter wheel means a shorter sidewall dimension for a given tire.

Since 35-inch-diameter tires are standard on the Sasquatch models and are a good upgrade size, I will use that diameter as an example. Referring back to the tire-pressure section earlier, reducing tire pressure off-road is a function of the tire sidewall height and other factors, including weight on the tire and tire-sidewall stiffness. As earlier stated, I generally use an 85-percent measurement for sidewall reduction for most off-road driving situations. A 35-inch-diameter tire on a 17-inch-diameter wheel has about a 9-inch sidewall height. Regardless of the tire brand or model, the ideal sidewall height is about 8 inches. If a 20-inch-diameter wheel is used, the sidewall height is now only 7.5 inches at full pressure $(35 - 20 \div 2)$. Reducing the sidewall height to the ideal 85-percent number is about a 6.9-inch sidewall height. This number requires a much higher tire pressure to make sure that the tire is not damaged when it is pinched between the wheel rim and the ground or

Beadlocks require proper installation and maintenance. Most beadlocks have 32 bolts that hold the outer ring in place. The bolts must be installed in the proper sequence and using the correct torque. I torque in

a rock. The higher tire pressure reduces the tire footprint and traction, increases ride harshness, and increases the risk of tire damage.

Width

Stock wheel widths on the Bronco are 7 to 8.5 inches. The stock wheel width works fine on tires up to about 9 inches wide, which includes 32- to 33-inch-diameter tires. Larger tires, such as those with a 12.50-inch section width, should use a wheel width of 8.0 to 9.0 inches

Offset and Backspacing

Wheel backspacing is critical on the Bronco 4x4s. Backspacing is measured from the back of the wheel rim to the surface where the wheel mounts to the hub. Too much backspacing with larger, wider tires can cause rubbing problems, as the front tires are turned near full lock and at the extremes of vertical suspension travel. Optimal backspacing for the Bronco is covered in the "Stock Wheel Specifications" chart.

Many aftermarket wheels have less backspacing than stock, which pushes the tire out farther. The smaller the backspacing measurement, the more the tire will stick out (away from the vehicle). This

BACK SPACING

OUTSIDE OF WHEEL

puts additional load on the wheel hubs and bearings. On a 9-inch-wide wheel with 4.5-inch backspacing, the center of the wheel interface with the hub is in the center of the wheel and the load on the wheel bearings is not

Wheel backspacing is measured from the back side of the wheel rim to where the wheel mounts on the face of the hub.

increased. Wider tires require less backspacing.

Spacers and Adapters

Wheel spacers that slip over the wheels studs can cause issues. Wheel adapters, which have built-in wheel studs and bolt onto the wheel studs on the hub, work better and are safer. Check the regulations in your state, as they are not legal in some states.

Wheel Care and Maintenance

Dirt, mud, sand, brake dust, and snow can corrode alloy wheel finishes. Clean the wheels thoroughly after off-road excursions. Use a good wheel cleaner and ceramic coating. Always follow the recommendations of the wheel manufacturer.

Lug-Bolt Torque

Correct wheel torque is critical for safety and to reduce the risk of damage to wheels, wheel studs, hubs, and lug nuts. The torque should be checked after every off-road run on rough terrain.

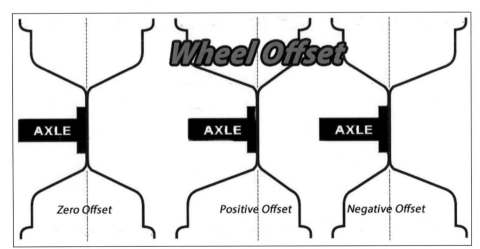

Wheel offset can be confusing. This graphic provides examples of positive, negative, and zero offset.

Tire Test Impressions

All of the tires listed here are quality products, as are many other tires. Most of the differences are small but can be significant in extreme conditions. All comments and ratings are my opinion. ∎

Nexen Roadian ATX

Category	Rating
Price	Moderate
Highway Noise	Low
Sidewall Stiffness	Medium Soft
Hill Climb Traction	Very Good
Hill Descent Traction	Very Good
Side-Slope Lateral Grip	Excellent
Grip in Big Ruts and Bumps	Excellent
Forward Grip Climbing Rocks	Very Good
Forward Grip Dropping off Rocks	Very Good
Lateral Grip on Side-Sloping Rocks	Excellent

Nexen Roadian ATX

Comments: • Overall excellent all-around off-road tire • Great for overlanding

Toyo Tires Open Country RT Trail

Category	Rating
Price	High
Highway Noise	Low
Sidewall Stiffness	Medium Hard
Hill Climb Traction	Very Good
Hill Descent Traction	Very Good
Side-Slope Lateral Grip	Good
Grip in Big Ruts and Bumps	Excellent
Forward Grip Climbing Rocks	Very Good
Forward Grip Dropping off Rocks	Very Good
Lateral Grip on Side-Sloping Rocks	Good

Toyo Open Country RT Trail

Comments: • Quality off-road tire • Excellent for overlanding • Durable

Falken Wild Peak AT03

Category	Rating
Price	High
Highway Noise	Medium High
Sidewall Stiffness	Hard
Hill Climb Traction	Very Good
Hill Descent Traction	Very Good
Side-Slope Lateral Grip	Very Good
Grip in Big Ruts and Bumps	Excellent
Forward Grip Climbing Rocks	Excellent
Forward Grip Dropping off Rocks	Excellent
Lateral Grip on Side-Sloping Rocks	Excellent

Falken Wild Peak AT03

Comments: • Quality off-road tire • Excellent for rocks and slick rock/granite • Durable

Mickey Thompson ATZ

Category	Rating
Price	High
Highway Noise	Medium High
Sidewall Stiffness	Hard
Hill Climb Traction	Excellent
Hill Descent Traction	Excellent
Side-Slope Lateral Grip	Excellent
Grip in Big Ruts and Bumps	Excellent
Forward Grip Climbing Rocks	Excellent
Forward Grip Dropping off Rocks	Excellent
Lateral Grip on Side-Sloping Rocks	Excellent

Mickey Thompson ATZ

Comments: • Excellent all around off-road tire • Excellent for rocks and slick rock/granite • Durable • An aggressive overlander

Hankook DynaPro XT

Category	Rating
Price	Medium High
Highway Noise	Medium
Sidewall Stiffness	Medium
Hill Climb Traction	Excellent
Hill Descent Traction	Excellent
Side-Slope Lateral Grip	Very good
Grip in Big Ruts and Bumps	Excellent
Forward Grip Climbing Rocks	Excellent
Forward Grip Dropping off Rocks	Excellent
Lateral Grip on Side-Sloping Rocks	Excellent

Hankook DynaPro XT

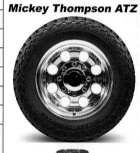

Comments: • Excellent all-around off-road tire • Excellent for overlanding • Good for rock crawling

Falken WildPeak MT

Category	Rating
Price	Medium High
Highway Noise	High
Sidewall Stiffness	High
Hill Climb Traction	Excellent
Hill Descent Traction	Excellent
Side-Slope Lateral Grip	Very good
Grip in Big Ruts and Bumps	Excellent
Forward Grip Climbing Rocks	Excellent
Forward Grip Dropping off Rocks	Excellent
Lateral Grip on Side-Sloping Rocks	Excellent

Falken WildPeak MT

Comments: • Excellent all around off-road tire
• Excellent for rock crawling

Toyo Tires Open Country MT

Category	Rating
Price	Medium High
Highway Noise	High
Sidewall Stiffness	Very good
Hill Climb Traction	Very good
Hill Descent Traction	Very good
Side-Slope Lateral Grip	Very good
Grip in Big Ruts and Bumps	Excellent
Forward Grip Climbing Rocks	Excellent
Forward Grip Dropping off Rocks	Excellent
Lateral Grip on Side-Sloping Rocks	Good

Toyo Open Country MT

Comments: • High quality • Excellent all-around off-road tire
• Good for overlanding • Good for rock crawling

Hankook DynaPro MT2

Category	Rating
Price	Medium High
Highway Noise	Medium high
Sidewall Stiffness	Medium
Hill Climb Traction	Excellent
Hill Descent Traction	Excellent
Side-Slope Lateral Grip	Excellent
Grip in Big Ruts and Bumps	Excellent
Forward Grip Climbing Rocks	Excellent
Forward Grip Dropping off Rocks	Excellent
Lateral Grip on Side-Sloping Rocks	Excellent

Hankook DynaPro MT2

Comments: • Excellent all-around off-road tire • Very good for overlanding • Excellent for rock crawling

Nexen Roadian MTX

Category	Rating
Price	Medium
Highway Noise	Medium high
Sidewall Stiffness	Medium soft
Hill Climb Traction	Excellent
Hill Descent Traction	Excellent
Side-Slope Lateral Grip	Excellent
Grip in Big Ruts and Bumps	Excellent
Forward Grip Climbing Rocks	Excellent
Forward Grip Dropping off Rocks	Excellent
Lateral Grip on Side-Sloping Rocks	Excellent

Nexen Roadian MTX

Comments: • Excellent all-around off-road tire
• Good for overlanding • Excellent for rock crawling
• Soft, flexy sidewalls considering that it's a load-range "F" design • Arguably the best-value MT tire available

Mickey Thompson Baja Boss MT

Category	Rating
Price	High
Highway Noise	Medium high
Sidewall Stiffness	Stiff
Hill Climb Traction	Excellent
Hill Descent Traction	Excellent
Side-Slope Lateral Grip	Excellent
Grip in Big Ruts and Bumps	Excellent
Forward Grip Climbing Rocks	Excellent
Forward Grip Dropping off Rocks	Excellent
Lateral Grip on Side-Sloping Rocks	Excellent

Mickey Thompson Baja Boss MT

Comments: • Excellent all-around off-road tire
• Excellent for rock crawling and extremely difficult terrain

SUSPENSION

Nearly all modern pickup trucks and SUVs come equipped with an independent front suspension and a solid rear axle setup. While an independent front suspension provides some advantages over a solid-axle front setup, several disadvantages also exist. The pros and cons of independent front suspension require further discussion, but first, let's look at the various tasks that each suspension component must undertake.

The new Bronco uses an independent front suspension system.

Vertical movement and longitudinal location on the front wheels is controlled by A-arm-style control arms. The A-arms allow some camber and caster adjustments. Coilover springs and shock absorbers are used. A front anti-roll (sway) bar helps control body roll. A front sway-bar disconnect is offered on some models, excluding the Wildtrak.

The independent front suspension reduces unsprung weight, which improves ride quality and handling characteristics. Unsprung weight consists of the weight that is not supported by the springs. This includes the wheels, tires hubs, brakes, half of the weight of the suspension control arms and half shafts (independent front suspension axles) in independent front suspension systems or the full weight of the axle and gear assembly on a solid-rear-axle system.

At the rear of the Bronco, a solid-axle assembly drives the vehicle. Vertical and longitudinal control uses a four-link suspension control-arm setup with a track bar that is used for lateral axle placement. Coil springs and shocks are used. Spring mounts on the front and rear shock absorbers are not adjustable to raise the chassis.

The Bronco utilizes an independent front suspension system that is ideal for high-speed desert adventures.

The downside of an independent front suspension is limited articulation, even with the front sway bar disconnected.

The Bronco Badlands suspension features Bilstein shocks. The coilover springs are fixed and not adjustable for ride height. (Photo Courtesy Ford Motor Company)

A track bar locates the solid rear axle laterally to keep the rear axle housing properly positioned. (Photo Courtesy Ford Motor Company)

All sixth-generation Broncos use a four-link trailing-arm rear suspension. The sway bar does not disconnect.

Suspension Components

The suspension systems on vehicles allow controlled vertical movement of the tires over irregularities on road surfaces and while negotiating corners. In addition, suspension provides stability by controlling body roll and allows a handling balance between front and rear tire traction by controlling where weight is transferred (front versus rear) while cornering.

Highway driving and off-road travel require similar characteristics but are not completely compatible. Highway driving generally utilizes a stiffer suspension because paved roads are usually smoother.

Off-road driving requires more ground clearance, more suspension travel, and a much softer suspension to allow the tires to stay on the road surface over a wide variety of ruts, bumps, rocks, and soft surfaces. Highway vehicles with off-road capabilities present a serious challenge to suspension engineers. Different vehicles from different manufacturers make a wide range of compromises, with characteristics that range from good on the highway and okay off-road to really good off-road and not so great on the highway.

Here is a summary of the major suspension components and what they do:

Springs

Springs support the weight of the vehicle. Increase the weight of a rig with your gear, and stiffer, taller springs will be needed to handle the additional weight. Springs also absorb bumps and ruts. In reality, springs absorb shock loads from road-surface irregularities. If springs absorb shock loads, what do shock

The Badlands model features the HOSS 2.0 system with Bilstein position-sensitive dampers (PSDs). (Photo Courtesy Ford Motor Company)

absorbers do? They dampen vibrations (oscillations), which is why the technical term for shock absorbers is "vibration dampers."

The most important job of the springs is to keep the tire contact patches on the road surface as much as possible as well as affecting ride comfort. If springs are too stiff, the ride is harsh and the tires often lose contact with the road surface. If springs are too soft, the vehicle will bottom out on the suspension or the ground, wallow, and feel unstable. Springs are used to lift a 4x4 for improved tire and ground clearance and more axle articulation. However, if the lift springs are too stiff, ride comfort is hurt, the ability of the springs to keep the tires on the ground is reduced, and articulation is reduced. Spring rates should be near stock or slightly stiffer.

Control Arms

Suspension control arms and linkages include trailing arms on solid axles or A-arms on independent suspensions. Suspension arms control the movement of the wheels and tires in vertical travel. They affect the amount of wheel travel and articulation. Independent suspension uses A-arm-style control arms. The geometry of the upper and lower control arms determines the lateral arc the wheel and tire travel. The relative lengths of the control arms affect the amount of up and down travel that is available, which affects articulation.

Trailing arms are used on solid axles to control the vertical travel of the wheels and tires. The longer the arms, the larger the arc of travel becomes. Longer arms mean that longitudinal movement is minimized during suspension travel. Longer arms also allow more axle articulation within the range of suspension travel up (compression or

All sixth-generation Bronco models use an A-arm upper control arm. Many aftermarket companies offer front upper and lower suspension arms for slightly improved geometry and enhanced strength. (Photo Courtesy Ford Motor Company)

bump travel) and down (extension or rebound travel).

Adjustable control arms allow suspension alignment. Caster, camber, and toe settings allow optimal geometry. Adjustable arms also allow the axles to be aligned so that they are square to the chassis and parallel to each other, which controls how well the vehicle tracks and steers.

Suspension Travel

While not a component, suspension travel dictates an off-road suspension system's performance. Several factors limit suspension travel, including spring height, stiffness, and design; shock-absorber travel; tire clearance in the fender wells; A-arm and control-arm travel limitations; and angularity on independent suspension axle-shaft joints.

Longer springs increase suspension travel if the other limitations are properly addressed to allow increased travel. Coilover springs and shocks may allow ride-height adjustments (raise or lower the body/chassis) with adjustable spring perches. They do not increase suspension travel unless the coilover spring and shock are longer and allow more travel. Raising the spring perch on a coilover will raise the vehicle (increase ground clearance) but will not increase vertical suspension travel. Raising the spring perch changes the ride height but will decrease "down" travel and increase "up" travel. Additional limitations on suspension travel affect independent front suspension systems more than solid-axle suspensions due to axle-shaft and tie-rod angle limitations.

Shock Absorbers (Vibration Dampers)

Shocks control the oscillations or bouncing of the springs. In other words, the shock dampens vibra-

tions of the spring. The vehicle will wallow and bounce if the shocks are too soft, and if the shocks are too stiff, it will cause an uncomfortable ride. The shock absorbers on many rigs are subject to extreme loads. High-quality shocks always perform better than the low-cost (often low-quality) shocks.

If a shock is too stiff, tire contact with the ground as well as articulation are reduced. If a shock is too short on a lifted 4x4, vertical travel as well as articulation are reduced.

Shock-absorber damping rates also control how quickly weight is transferred from one tire to another when cornering, braking, accelerating, and when the axles are articulating. This affects transitional handling balance and also how quickly weight moves from one tire to the tire that is still loaded when a rock or bump is encountered. Shock rates are controlled by valves that allow fluid to bleed. Different valve sets come into play at different shaft speeds. Some shocks use additional bypass bleed ports within the bore of the shock.

Different valves and bypasses control damping rates for different shaft and piston speeds. This allows fine-tuning of valving to accommodate for various situations—from driving twisty mountain roads to rock crawling and rolling bumps in the desert. Valving in a shock should be compatible with the loads to which the shock is subjected. What works on a stock 4x4 vehicle is not adequate for a heavily-laden overlanding rig or the slow movements when rock crawling.

Lifted rigs need longer shocks to take advantage of the increased spring travel and articulation. When selecting a lift kit for your Bronco, purchase one that has both springs

The HOSS 3.0 package on the Wildtrak model features Fox internal-bypass dampers (shocks) and a taller ride height suspension to accommodate taller tires.

and shocks as a coordinated package along with any necessary control arms, bushings, and other hardware. Shock travel should be limited in extension so that the shock cannot fully extend, which can damage the piston and internal valving. In compression, bump stops are used to limit travel so that damage to the shock internals is avoided.

Sway Bars (Anti-Roll Bars)

Sway bars (also called anti-roll bars) control body roll when cornering by twisting as weight transfers laterally in a corner. The sway bars also affect handling balance by affecting where weight transfers (more front or more rear weight transfer) while cornering. However, for off-road travel, sway bars greatly reduce the ability of the axles to articulate by reducing travel. Essentially, sway bars limit suspension travel. In addition, sway bars increase ride harshness in

The rear sway bar, which is much softer than the front sway bar, does not disconnect.

the bumpy conditions encountered off-road.

Disconnecting the sway bars helps articulation off-road but negatively affects handling and stability on the road. The front sway bar is much stiffer than the rear. For this reason, disconnecting only the front bar is necessary. Some Bronco models use an electric front sway-bar disconnect. Other models have attaching bolts on the sway-bar end links that can be removed fairly easily when going off-road.

A mechanical sway-bar disconnect requires the removal of a pin on each end to disconnect the bar. The Precision Works quick-disconnect sway-bar end links for the Ford Bronco 2021 (and newer) feature a billet 6061 aluminum body, quality heim joints with disconnects, and adjustable-length end links. (Photo Courtesy Precision Works)

The front sway bar on most Bronco models with the Sasquatch package uses an electric sway-bar disconnect. A great feature of the Bronco's front sway-bar disconnect is the ability to disconnect while under load. The case on the bar in the foreground of the photo is the sway-bar-disconnect mechanism. (Photo Courtesy Ford Motor Company)

The patent-pending airLYNX from Apex Design was designed to make disconnecting the sway bar much faster and easier. The Bronco airLYNX provides the ability to tune how much force your sway bar is applying by simply airing up or airing down your links. Broncos offer 8 inches of stock wheel travel. The Apex airLYNX delay engagement to the stock sway bar when at 0 psi. They are fully disconnected for the first 3 inches of wheel travel. Beyond the first 3 inches of wheel travel, they produce a reduced rate of engagement (or force) that is being applied by the sway bar. (Photo Courtesy Apex Design)

The AntiRock sway bars from RockJock 4x4 allow full axle articulation without disconnecting the bars. Rather than disconnect just the front sway bar with no roll resistance at the front, the AntiRock system maintains a balance of roll control for off-road use. (Photo Courtesy RockJock 4x4)

In addition, aftermarket sway-bar disconnects provide a means to easily disconnect the front sway bar for improved articulation. One of the best solutions for improved off-road axle articulation uses sway bars designed for optimal off-road performance. The RockJock Anti-Rock off-road sway bars provide great articulation with balanced roll resistance front to rear, and they do not require disconnecting when venturing off-road.

How Suspension Works

This section covers suspension travel and axle articulation.

Suspension Travel

Lift kits using taller springs (as opposed to spacers) and longer shocks with more travel increase suspension travel. More travel improves traction by allowing the tire contact patches to remain on the ground over rough terrain. The downside to independent front suspension when taller springs are

While suspension travel is good on all Bronco models, the lack of a sway-bar disconnect on the Wildtrak model limits down travel in ruts and bumps. Articulation is also limited. The left front tire here is nearly lifting off the road surface on a moderate bump.

installed is that it increases the angle of the axle shafts and tie-rods. When the chassis is lifted on an independent front suspension system, the axle shafts operate at a steeper angle, putting additional strain on the constant velocity (CV) joints. This accelerates wear and makes the joints more prone to failure. The steering tie-rods also take on greater angles, which also increases wear and makes failure more likely. The stock tie-rods on the Bronco are prone to failure.

Axle Articulation

Axle articulation is the ability of the axle or the axles (on independent front suspension) to rotate vertically with as much travel as possible to help keep tires on the ground over rocks, bumps, and ruts. Independent front suspension systems, such as those that are found on the Bronco, severely limit axle articulation at the front of the vehicle. The axles swing on an independent front suspension setup with pivot points at the center differential housing and at the wheel hubs. The shorter axles, which swing in a much smaller arc, limit articulation (compared to a solid axle). Reduced articulation leads to tires being lifted off the road surface earlier than they would with a solid-axle setup.

Axle articulation affects tire traction and vehicle stability. Articulation allows the axles to move in the largest possible arc. This allows the body to stay more level over large obstacles, such as rocks, ruts, and bumps. Good articulation not only improves vehicle stability but also

tire traction by keeping all four tires in contact with the ground. On the Bronco, as well as any independent front suspension–equipped 4x4, the short front axles minimize the ability of the front end to articulate.

Factors affecting axle articulation include sway bars, spring rates, suspension travel, and the pivot arc of the suspension. Sway bars minimize body roll when cornering. They also minimize axle articulation. Taller springs allow more travel. Shock absorbers that are too short for the springs limit travel (as does the sway bar). Sway-bar disconnects improve travel for off-road driving.

Free rotational movement of the front and rear axles allow the tire contact patches to stay on the road or trail surface over uneven terrain. This improves traction, helps stabilize the vehicle, and reduces the likelihood of suspension damage if the airborne tire/wheel/suspension slams back to the ground. Without good articulation, tires can lift off the ground in moderate to extreme rock-crawling situations and terrain with large

ruts and bumps. It is important to keep the tire contact patches on the ground as long as possible, even if the load is minimal on one tire.

When the tire lifts off the ground, it must return at some point. Often, the tire/wheel will return to earth harshly, which can damage the suspension and create a situation with reduced stability. Increased suspension travel and less resistance to body roll improves axle articulation. Suspension lifts with proper spring rates improve articulation. Sway bars limit articulation, which is why front sway-bar disconnects are important. Disconnecting the front sway bar allows more suspension travel, which allows the best axle articulation. Rear sway bars are very light by comparison, so a disconnect is unnecessary.

Suspension lifts allow more axle articulation as long as the front sway bar is disconnected or aftermarket sway bars are used. Bump stops should always be used to keep compression travel limited so that the springs and shocks do not bottom out. Limit the rebound travel to keep

Lifting a tire off the ground (as seen here) is not a big deal mechanically, but it can be unnerving to newcomers and especially to passengers.

Loren Healey and Vaughn Gitten Jr. operate the Fun-Haver Off-Road aftermarket company, which specializes in sixth-generation Bronco upgrades. The team also competes in the King of the Hammers event in Johnson Valley, California. Healey had the 2024 King of the Hammers event won until an inexpensive part failed about a mile from the finish of the grueling event. This Fun-Haver Off-Road Bronco is a customer version that is flying across the desert at a high rate of speed. (Photo Courtesy Fun-Haver Off-Road)

Bilstein offers several shock-absorber options for sixth-generation Broncos. The Bronco Badlands edition features Bilstein position-sensitive dampers (PSDs) from the factory. The Bilstein 6112 shocks for the Bronco are shown here. (Photo Courtesy Bilstein)

The Bronco Wildtrak features the Fox internal-bypass shock that perform great in high-speed ruts and bumps. The dust obscures the severity of the whoop-de-doos here, but the rear bump travel and front extension travel indicates the Bronco is cresting a good size bump at speed. The suspension is doing its job of keeping the body level.

the springs seated and the shocks from being fully extended during full extension or rebound travel. Shock absorbers can be damaged if they are fully compressed or extended.

Shock Absorbers

Shock absorbers actually dampen vibrations, and springs absorb shocks. When a tire encounters a bump, the suspension spring compresses, absorbing the load and softening the impact. In other words, it absorbs the shock. The shock absorber, which is technically called a vibration damper, controls the movements of the spring. The most important job of a shock is to stop the spring from oscillating when driving on uneven terrain. If a shock absorber is dead (no longer working), the spring will continue to bounce up and down until friction internal to the spring and control arm friction stops the oscillation.

For off-road applications, a shock works overtime, especially on rough roads with washboard sections and whoops. A weak shock will allow the tire contact patch to bounce off the road surface in these conditions. If the shock valving is too stiff, the chassis/body will move considerably because the shocks are not absorbing the movement and the body will move vertically, causing a very rough ride and making the vehicle unstable and feel skittish over the bumps. Properly valved and tuned shocks improve traction and ride quality in harsh conditions. In addition, good shocks allow smooth articulation in the bumps and allow tires to conform to rocks in extreme rock crawling situations.

Controlling vertical wheel/tire movement on independent front suspension vehicles, such as the Bronco, require less-extreme shock valving compared to a solid-axle front suspension. Fewer compromises are nec-

essary. For this reason, independent front suspension–equipped vehicles, such as the Bronco, offer better ride comfort on the highway and on rough surfaces on the dirt, especially at higher speeds.

Shock absorbers provide damping in both compression and extension travel. Compression is also referred to as bump travel, while extension is often referred to as rebound travel. Valving rates are different for bump and rebound. The damping force generated by the valving in the shock also varies as the shock-absorber shaft speed changes. High-speed situations, which would be found in the desert or on rough roads, cause rapid movements of the suspension. Rock crawling and driving in deep ruts and big bumps cause much slower movement of the suspension, resulting in slower shock shaft speeds. A variety of valves and bypasses internal to the shock control the dampening stiffness in both compression and extension travel and various shock-absorber shaft speeds.

Types

Shock absorbers are available in three types: twin tube, monotube, and bypass. The twin-tube shock is generally the type that is found as original equipment or as an original-equipment replacement shock. Twin-tube shocks are very inexpensive, but performance is limited. They tend to overheat easily in bumpy conditions. Overheating reduces the viscosity of the hydraulic oil in the shock, which reduces the ability of the shock to continue functioning properly. Twin-tube shocks wear quickly, especially in the harsh environment of off-roading. Twin-tube shocks easily overheat on rough roads and are also prone to breaking the shaft or the welds on the mounting points.

Monotube shocks provide better performance and durability. The valving of a monotube shock allows better control in more extreme conditions. Heat dissipation is improved, and monotube shocks are less prone to failure. Most monotube shocks are gas-charged with nitrogen. This helps with damping and heat dissipation. Some higher-end monotube shocks use a valve for the gas, which allows pressure adjustments that change the damping characteristics for various off-road driving situations.

Shock technology has improved significantly over the last few years with the advent of the bypass shock. Shock absorbers use a piston in the shock tube that compresses oil

Fox offers several shock options for the Bronco. The Fox external-bypass shocks with coilover springs allow ride-height adjustments. As with most high-end shocks, these are rebuildable. The smaller-diameter springs create more clearance during suspension travel. (Photo Courtesy Shock Surplus)

during shock travel. A series of orifices and valves within the piston determine the damping force. On high-end shocks, these valves can be altered by disassembling the shock or with external adjustment screws or knobs. This changes the resistance produced by the shock. The damping rate of the shock increases as the speed of the piston shaft increases. All shock absorbers are shaft-speed sensitive.

Bypass shocks utilize a series of valves (openings) in the body of the shock, which allows the oil to bypass the piston. These bypasses can be adjusted to soften the ride for a variety of off-road conditions. Near the ends of the piston travel in both compression and rebound, oil is forced to flow through the orifices in the piston, which increases the rate of the shock as it nears its limits of travel. This helps keep the shock from bottoming out in harsh road conditions. Bypass shocks offer external adjustment, usually for rebound travel but sometimes for both bump and rebound (compression and extension). Bypass shocks can be fine-tuned for nearly any condition—from low-speed rock crawling to high-speed desert racing.

Bypass shocks can be internal or external. An internal bypass means that the bypasses are maintained within the body of the shock. External-bypass shocks have bypass tubes external to the shock body. There is little difference in performance. The one advantage to an internal-bypass shock is the compact nature of the shock without external tubes. This allows the internal-bypass shock to be used in coilover setups.

Remote-reservoir shocks can be the monotube design or the bypass design. The remote reservoir can be attached to the shock body or can use a hose to allow remote mounting locations. The remote mounting allows more options for clearance. The remote reservoir provides a larger quantity of oil, which circulates through the shock for improved cooling and less chance of cavitation.

OEM Shocks and Suspension

Ford offers the HOSS 1.0, 2.0, 3.0, and 4.0 suspension systems.

HOSS 1.0

The HOSS 1.0 system is standard on the base, Big Bend, Black Diamond, and Outer Banks models. It features a 190-mm independent front suspension axle; a 220-mm solid rear axle; 1-zone damping; and a base-level steering rack, steering gear, and tie-rod system.

It is capable and comfortable. Armed to the teeth with a set of conventional house-tuned Hitachi twin-tube dampers, this suspension is ready for just about everything under the sun—as long as you are not in a hurry. More gas means more force applied, and that's when limits are felt.

It features twin forged alloy A-arms with long-travel coilover springs, a 190-mm independent front suspension axle, a 220-mm solid rear axle with long-travel, and variable-rate coilover springs. If you're headed off the beaten path, this provides good performance.

HOSS 2.0

The HOSS 2.0 system is standard on Badlands, Wildtrak, Everglades, Heritage, Heritage Limited, and Sasquatch-equipped Broncos. It features a 210-mm independent front suspension axle, a 220-mm solid rear axle, and three-zone damping. It is offered in two steering rack, steering gear, and tie-rod systems (base and Sasquatch) and in two track widths (base and Sasquatch). The four-door Sasquatch began offering a rear stabilizer bar in 2022.

For 33-inch and 35-inch off-road fans, the Badlands, Everglades, Wildtrak, and trims equipped with the Sasquatch package ship with Bilstein monotube dampers that have external piggyback bypass reservoirs. These 3-zone, position-sensitive shocks are tuned for resisting bottoming out or donkey-kicking at full suspension droop. External reservoirs pump up the oil capacity within the shock for greater endurance against shock fade, and the end stop control valve (ESCV) technology improves handling and ride.

This suspension system also qualifies the Bronco for a 210-mm independent front suspension axle and half-shaft upgrade. The 35-inch tire Sasquatch package–equipped vehicles gain additional upgrades in the form of a heavy-duty steering rack, motor, gear, and tie-rods to further combat the forces of the larger and heavier 35-inch tires. The available sway-bar disconnect allows mogul aficionados to further stretch out the suspension to navigate wildly uneven terrain.

HOSS 3.0

The HOSS 3.0 system was a Wildtrak option in 2022 and became standard in 2023. It features Fox 2.5-inch internal-bypass dampers, the Ford Performance severe-duty upgraded steering rack from the Bronco Raptor, a 210-mm independent front suspension axle, a 220-mm solid rear axle, and five-zone damping. It also includes the Raptor motor, upgraded tie-rods, the Sasquatch steering ratio, a 25-mm offset track width, and a rear stabilizer bar on two-door and four-door versions.

High-speed desert driving improves with the 5-zone, rate-sensitive 2.5-inch Fox Racing internal-bypass shocks that were available for the Wildtrak.

These trophy truck–inspired, fully rebuildable, nitrogen-charged shocks are siblings to the race-proven Fox shocks that are available for the F-150 Raptor and Bronco Raptor. Frame-mounted, external-remote, piggyback reservoirs front and rear exceed the HOSS 2.0 equipment with even greater heat dissipation capacity

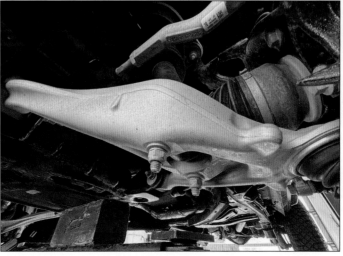

The stock upper and lower control arms are a cast alloy. While strong, aftermarket tubular A-arms provide more strength and often improved geometry. The springs on the Wildtrak are not adjustable for ride height.

and fade resistance. The Wildtrak is equipped with the Ford Performance severe-duty steering rack for the Bronco Raptor, with Sasquatch close-ratio steering gear ratios. The tie-rod ends are further upgraded to cope with greater loads.

HOSS 4.0

The HOSS 4.0 suspension system is standard on the Bronco Raptor. It features Live Valve 3.1 internal-bypass, semi-active dampers; positive-sensitive damping; integrated front reservoirs; and remote reservoirs in the rear.

Optimal Shock Valving

Shock absorbers must operate in a wide range of situations. Non-adjustable or rebuildable shocks are optimal for one type of driving. Off-road performance may or may not be a priority. For this reason, bypass shocks have become very popular, as valving rate adjustments are easily made.

Shock Length and Travel

When lifting a Bronco, the shock length and travel must be taken into account. Lift kits with shocks often come with shock extension brackets to allow for the lift springs. These brackets allow clearance but not the additional travel that allows greater axle articulation. It is best to install a lift kit, which includes shocks that are matched to the lift height. Proper-length shocks allow full travel and articulation and will not hinder the improved performance offered by the lift.

Shaft Diameter

One indication of a shock absorber's durability is the diameter of the shaft. Less-expensive aftermarket shocks have shaft diameters in the 0.5- to 0.6-inch range. Premium shocks have larger shaft diameters, up to 0.875 inch. Shafts can bend, and the mounting end welds are weak points that can break in difficult terrain.

Shock Body Diameter and Piston Area

The diameter of the shock body dictates the piston size and area. The advantage to larger shock bodies and pistons is improved cooling and better control of valving. Shock-body diameters range from 2 to 3 inches. The most common diameter for most monotube shocks is 2 inches. While larger shocks have some advantages, the 2-inch body shocks offer great off-road performance for a reasonable cost.

Bump Stops and Travel Limit Straps

Shock absorbers can be damaged when they are fully compressed or fully extended, especially if the load is high. Bump stops limit shock travel during compression or bump travel. The bump stop, as the name implies, keeps the shock from bottoming out by limiting travel. Stock bump stops are made of a hard rubber compound which does little to dampen the impact, but the possibility of damage is limited. Many aftermarket lift kits

While independent front suspension offers superior performance in rough terrain, such as washboard sections or desert whoop-de-dos, uneven ruts and bumps negatively impact the Bronco due to a lack of articulation. The lifting of tires and then crashing back to the surface can damage the shocks and possibly the suspension. Slow speeds and skilled driving help to alleviate this issue in the rough stuff.

The stock Bronco Wildtrak possesses good suspension up travel (bump travel). Extension travel is limited by the lack of a sway-bar disconnect. Sway-bar disconnects are available from the aftermarket. However, longer-travel shock absorbers may be needed to accommodate the extra "down" travel.

provide taller bump stops to compensate for the increased length of the new shock. These bump stops are made from metal or hard rubber.

Hydraulic bump stops are generally used on solid-axle systems (as opposed to independent front suspension). Hydraulic bump stops function similar to a simplified shock absorber to dampen the impact when the bump stop is engaged. Hydraulic bump stops help control axle and wheel movement near the limits of bump travel, but the effect is fairly small compared to the hard-material bump stops. Most bypass shocks have internal bump stops or increased-rate valving as the shock nears the extreme of bump travel.

Limiting rebound or extension travel is less critical. The loads are smaller, but limiting rebound travel is necessary when the spring could become unseated from the spring perch due to excessive travel. If the spring unseats, it could fall out of the perch or become unseated from the indexed spring perch (at a minimum). Limit straps are made from web material similar to a seat belt. The strap bolts to the chassis at one end and the axle at the other end.

Coilovers

The stock springs on the sixth-generation Broncos mount over the shock absorbers, making them a coilover setup. The spring diameter is fairly large compared to most aftermarket coilover systems. The stock spring location on the shocks is not easily adjusted for lifting the Bronco.

Aftermarket coilover systems generally use a smaller-diameter spring. The smaller spring takes up less room, allowing more clearance. In addition, aftermarket coilovers

The Fox competition shocks feature reservoirs and external bypasses, and they are adjustable. The shocks use threaded collars to easily make ride height adjustments. Note the billet aluminum upper control arm.

offer some adjustment for raising (or lowering) the chassis. Some coilover shock bodies use grooves in the body with a snap ring to hold the spring in place. Several grooves allow multiple heights. A spring compressor is needed to remove the spring to make ride-height adjustments.

Other coilover setups use a threaded sleeve over the shock body with a threaded adjuster ring and a lock ring to position the spring. Spanner wrenches are used to adjust the height of the adjuster ring on the shock body to the desired lift height. The lock ring is then tightened to the adjuster ring to keep the spring at the desired height. Adjustments can be made without removing the spring.

Solid Axles versus Independent Suspension

This comparison covers on-highway handling, the ride on rough surfaces, ground clearance, and suspension lift limitations.

On-Highway Handling

Independent suspensions, at least on the front, provide superior handling and ride comfort on the highway.

The adjustable-ride-height bypass King coilover shocks provide great damping for exceptional off-road handling in desert terrain. Note the steel tubular upper control arm and the billet aluminum lower control arm.

The geometry of an independent suspension allows better camber angle control. The tire will better conform to the road surface with independent suspension. This improves cornering

The independent front suspension on all Broncos improves on-highway handling and ride comfort. The Bronco Raptor, with increased track width over standard sixth-generation Broncos, offers even better highway handling.

The sixth-generation Bronco was created to tackle this kind of desert terrain.

traction and overall handling characteristics. Solid axles experience more camber change when cornering, resulting in slightly reduced cornering capability,

Ride on Rough Surfaces

Independent suspension systems reduce unsprung weight significantly. Unsprung weight is the weight that is not supported by the springs. Unsprung weight includes wheels, tires, brakes, hubs, and axles. Only half of the weight of components, such as axle shafts and suspension control arms, are unsprung on independent suspension setups. The reduced unsprung weight on independent suspension systems improves ride quality over bumps, through ruts, and over small rocks. The ride improves on washboard roads and whoop-de-dos as well. Independent suspensions perform better than solid-axle systems on easy terrain, with superior ride comfort and slightly better traction on rough terrain.

Ground Clearance

Suspension lifts are installed to gain additional ground clearance, which mostly means fitting taller tires. A lift with stock-size tires offers only marginal increases in ground clearance, mostly under the third members of independent suspension systems. While this certainly helps, taller tires will give the most increase in ground clearance.

Most SUV-based rigs are severely limited to tire size increases due to fender and chassis clearance limitations. This is especially true for vans, such as the Ford Transit and Mercedes-Benz Sprinter. At the other extreme, vehicles, such as the Jeep Wrangler and the Ford Bronco (full size), allow more room for larger tires but are still limited, even with a lift. The ideal lift is the smallest lift that

The Bronco Wildtrak with the Sasquatch package and 35-inch-tall tires has good ground clearance in stock form. A 2-inch lift is about the maximum lift that is practical on the Bronco due to the angles of the drive (half) shafts. A 2-inch lift is enough to fit 37-inch-tall tires.

allows the fitment of taller tires that fit within the stock fenders and do not interfere with the frame, suspension, or inner body panels.

Additional lift raises the center of gravity, making the rig more "tippy." One important lift consideration requires determining the load that is added to the vehicle from passengers, supplies, recovery items, and other gear. Stiffer springs may be needed just to return the vehicle back to the original ride height and ground clearance.

Suspension Lift Limitations

Lift heights for rigs with front and rear solid-axle assemblies are more easily lifted higher than rigs with independent front suspension. Solid-axle vehicles (Jeep Wranglers, early Broncos and Chevy Blazers, and many trucks, including the Ram Power Wagon) can generally be lifted up to 5 inches to allow larger tires and significant increases in ground clearance. A practical limit is 4 inches to keep the center of gravity at a more sane level and reduce the rollover risk.

Independent suspension systems cause another set of issues. The biggest concern for lifts on an independent suspension is the angle of the driveshafts. The driveshafts that run from the ring-and-pinion center section to the wheel hubs are fairly level at rest on a stock rig. Lifting the ride height changes the angle of the axle shafts so that they run downhill from the ring-and-pinion housing. Two problems occur.

First, the increased angle induces more stress on the joints that allow the axle shafts to swing up and down. The higher the lift, the more stress is put on the shafts and the more likely a joint could experience

The custom billet aluminum upper control arm and smaller-diameter suspension spring allows fitment of the Fox competition external-bypass, remote-reservoir shocks. This setup is on the Fun-Haver Off-Road *Bronco racing in the King of the Hammers 4600 stock class.*

The Fun-Haver Off-Road *race Bronco uses adjustable coilover springs and shocks. The custom rear sway bar is adjustable to help adjust handling characteristic for high-speed desert runs. Note the heavily trussed 9-inch rear axle.*

accelerated wear or fail. Lifts of more than 2.5 inches place excessive loads on the rotating joints. Pickups with tall lifts (up to 8 to 10 inches) use kits with a drop bracket to lower the ring-and-pinion center section housing and bring axle shaft angles closer to stock. However, the additional ground clearance is lost.

A second negative factor affects suspension travel. The angles of the axle shafts and suspension control arms changes. The downward angle of the components reduces "down" (extension or rebound) travel while increasing "up" travel. The amount of total travel remains the same (assuming adequate tire clearance in

Threaded shock bodies allow easy ride-height adjustments on coilover shocks.

Fabricated steel-tube upper control arms from Chaos Fabrication add considerable strength. The tilt of the upper control arm adds anti-dive to the front suspension, which limits dive under heavy braking. The coilover springs are from Eibach, which is a premier spring manufacturer. The adjustable bypass shocks are from Radflo.

Even a moderate 2-inch lift on a Bronco causes very noticeable angulation on the lower control arm, drive (half) shaft and steering tie-rod. The lift places additional strain on the axle CV joints and reduces the "down" travel of the suspension. The angle of the tie-rod also places a slight bending force on the steering rack.

the fenders). The percentage of "up" versus "down" travel changes, which hurts axle articulation even more. This applies to coilover springs as well as conventional springs.

Coilover spring/shock systems with a threaded collar provide easy ride-height adjustments. A corner of the rig can be raised or lowered to gain ground clearance, fit larger tires, and level the vehicle. However, when the ride height is raised (often called preloading the spring), extension or rebound travel reduces while "up" travel (bump or compression) is increased.

The ultimate solution for lifting a sixth-generation Bronco (although it is expensive) uses the 74Weld portal axles. These axles use a gearset at the wheel hub, which lifts the vehicle without a suspension spring lift. The stock springs and shocks can be used as the control arms and steering tie-rods remain at stock angles, eliminating the problems of lifting with springs. The travel remains the same as stock, and ride quality is stock, but the portal hubs create a nearly 4-inch lift.

In addition, the four gears in the portal hub increase the gearing by a 1.22:1 ratio. On a Sasquatch package with a 4.7:1 axle ratio, the effective axle ratio at the wheels is now 5.73:1. The lift and gear will allow the use of a 39- or even a 40-inch tire, but 40-inch-or-larger tires may require more fender clearance. The 74Weld portals have been proven in competition at the brutal King of the Hammers

race in the *Fun-Haver Off-Road* 4400 class Broncos of Vaughn Gitten Jr. and Loren Healy. Several Jeep competitors, such as Casey Currie and Jason Scherer, also use the 74Weld portals. They have proven to be extremely durable. Combine the 74Weld portals with the 74Weld billet-aluminum steering rack, and the result is a bulletproof off-roader that is capable in the most extreme trails.

Camburg manufactures many suspension components for the sixth-generation Broncos. This fabricated steel-tube upper control arm offers exceptional strength and improved suspension geometry.

Shock	Overview	Pros	Cons
Bilstein B8 5100 monotube 0-2.9-inch set (2021–2023 Ford Bronco four-door)	One of the best-selling shocks for the truck, SUV, and Jeep market, the Bilstein 5100 excels at daily drivability mixed with off-road capability. The Bilstein 5100 for the Bronco allows for ride height adjustment on all four corners, using the factory coil springs.	• Able to lift all four corners using stock springs • Great off-road-capable shock upgrade • More comfortable (than stock) on the road and for mild to moderate speeds off-road than the stock Bilstein ESCV • Durable, long lasting • Improved handling on- and off-road • Heavy duty, tow/haul capable	• Firmer than the Hitachi shocks used on lesser models • Performance shock at higher price • May be too soft for some drivers on 35-inch and 37-inch tires

Recommended Use: Daily Driver

Additional Notes: Softer (on pavement/easy trails) than the HOSS 2.0 ESCV shocks

Bilstein 6100 60-mm 0-2.6-inch set (2021–2023 Ford Bronco four-door)	A new addition to Bilstein's arsenal, the 6112 and 6100 shocks are equipped with a massive 60-mm active piston and 2.6-inch shock body, providing exceptional off-road capability and handling. This shock is aimed at the adventurer, off-roader, and overlander who sees a lot of dirt but also doesn't want to sacrifice daily-driver comfort.	• Able to lift all four corners using stock springs • 60-mm piston (best in class) • Price-to-shock ratio through the roof (2.6-inch shock and spring less expensive than 2-inch coilovers) • Massive off-road ride upgrade, improved road handling and comfort • Long lasting, durable, serviceable	• Does not come preassembled from Bilstein • Requires coil-spring compressor for installation

Recommended Use: Daily Driver, Hauling/Towing, and Off-Road

Additional Notes: 6100 shocks can only be used on Broncos with HOSS 2.0 suspension (Models with HOSS 1.0 need 6112s)

Eibach Pro-Truck Coilover Kit (2021-and-newer Ford Bronco)	Eibach's Pro-Truck coilover system for the 2021-and-newer Bronco is a plug-and-play upgrade to the handling and performance of these rigs. These are ride-height adjustable while on the vehicle, which makes adaptation easy for larger tires or load-hauling requirements.	• Improved comfort over the HOSS 2.0 ESCV shock package on the road and easy trails • Ride-height adjustable, even while on the vehicle • Built for longevity, 1-million-mile warranty by Eibach	• None

Recommended Use: Hauling/Towing

Additional Notes: This is a great upgrade in handling and performance compared to the Bilstein 5100

Icon EXP 2.5 Shocks	The Icon Vehicle Dynamics 2.5 EXP series shocks utilize an all-aluminum body with snap-ring grooves to provide a range of height adjustment. These shocks use the factory springs and top mounts, providing an inexpensive entry point for more performance.	• Inexpensive 2.5 performance shock • Uses factory coil springs and top mounts • Ride height adjustable to provide lift for larger tires or heavier loads • Improved handling over 2.0 shocks to give more confidence under load or towing	• Requires a coil-spring compressor to install • Cannot be ride-height adjusted while on the vehicle

Recommended Use: Hauling/Towing

Shock Surplus Bronco Shock Recommendations *By Sean Bowman Shocksurplus.com*			*continued*
Shock	**Overview**	**Pros**	**Cons**
King Shocks System (2021-and-newer Ford Bronco) 	King's off-road shocks for your application are unmatched in ride comfort and performance, offering great tuning out of the box. These shocks really excel in high-speed environments and aggressive terrain, for serious off-road enthusiasts.	• One of the highest-performing shocks available for OEM applications • Serviceable, rebuildable, and custom tuning is available • Compression adjustment and reservoir options • Blue color	• Lacking some features that competitors have
Recommended Use: Off-Road			
Fox 2.5 Performance Elite Coilovers set (2021-and newer Ford Bronco) 	Stepping up to the Fox 2.5 Performance Elite series shocks brings significant improvements in comfort and ride control. The increased size of the 2.5-inch shock offers increased shock oil and lower operating pressures and allows high-speed driving on aggressive terrain while maintaining great control of the vehicle through race-level tuning.	• Huge improvement to road comfort and off-road handling in one package • Adjustable, reservoir options serviceable, rebuildable, custom tuning available • Excellent handling in high-speed environments	• Requires servicing between 30,000–50,000 miles for optimal performance
Recommended Use: Off-Road			
Icon Vehicle Dynamics Stage 3 Overview 	Icon's 2.5 coilovers have proven to provide substantial support at higher off-road speeds and dealing with increased loads for long-range adventures and overlanding. As a high-performance shock, handling feels great on larger tires and body roll is reduced without much sacrifice to comfort.	• High performance means these are built for speed and support, • Serviceable, rebuildable, re-tunable to optimize ride behavior • Optimal for drivers who want handling and performance	• Requires servicing by 40,000 to 60,000 miles, (depending on use/abuse)
Recommended Use: Off-Road			
Additional Notes: Sportier ride characteristics sometimes leaves customers wanting more comfort			

STEERING AND ALIGNMENT

Of all the issues that cause problems on the trail (short of a crash), steering failure creates a substantial headache. Vehicle recoveries with broken steering require a great deal of work to overcome. The sixth-generation Bronco, unfortunately, suffers from a weak steering system where tie-rods are prone to failure, which can also damage the steering rack and destroy the CV joints on the front axles. Fortunately, the Bronco aftermarket has stepped up by offering much stronger tie-rods and other steering upgrades.

Steering systems allow maneuvering on and off the highway, unless a component of the steering system fails. The rigors of off-road driving place large loads on the steering system of any 4x4 vehicle. Even 4x4s with a solid front axle can experience failure on the extremely rough, rutted, and rock-strewn trails.

Steering System

Tie-rods, steering arms, and steering boxes can wear rapidly from the stresses of off-roading. Parts can also fail, rendering steering control nonexistent. If a steering-system component fails at low speed, it's a scary situation. At higher speeds, a steer-

ing failure is a terrifying catastrophe. Broken steering results in extremely difficult and potentially expensive vehicle recoveries. Ask how I know! Failure of any steering system component is dangerous. It is something to avoid.

Upgraded steering components, especially tie-rods, steering arms, and drag links (on solid front axle setups), reduce the possibility of failures. Independent front suspension systems use a rack-and-pinion steering box connected to tie-rods which push against the steering arms to turn the front wheels and tires. On paved and smooth surfaces, the tie-rods on independent front suspension vehicles experience fairly small loads. However, off-road, given the extreme erosion on most of the dirt roads and trails, the loads on the tie-rods increase dramatically.

Most independent front suspension–equipped 4x4s, including the Bronco, use small tie-rods, which are fine for the highway but not so much for off-road use. Since the launch of the new Bronco, the platform has been plagued by tie-rod failures. Tie-rod failure, in addition to being very scary, often results in damage to other components, such as front

This sequence of video stills shows a tie-rod failure in progress on a Bronco. In the first image, the tie-rod is intact. The front tires have just lost sideways grip, forcing the Bronco to slide into a big rock. In the second photo, the left front tire hit the rock, causing the left tie-rod to bend to about a 30-degree angle—not good! In the final image, the left tire has turned to the right (unseen in the photo), but the right front tire is pointing straight ahead.

axle shafts, CV joints, hubs, etc. As is often the case in the off-road arena, the 4x4 aftermarket has stepped up, offering beefier tie-rods and other critical components. It is highly recommended that aftermarket tie-rods (at the very least) be installed on the sixth-generation Bronco before any serious off-roading takes place.

Independent front suspension steering systems vary somewhat from solid-axle front ends. While the components are similar and perform the same functions, the mechanical aspects are considerably different. Where the solid-axle setup uses a single tie-rod with a drag link to transfer steering motions from the steering box to the wheel hubs, an independent suspension system uses two tie-rods, linking each end of the rack-and-pinion steering box to the front wheels.

Each system has advantages and disadvantages. Rack-and-pinion steering on independent front suspension provides superior handling and feel on the highway. Off-road, the independent suspension system is more fragile. Both systems leave something to be desired off-road. More weight, larger tires, and more difficult terrain make the rack-and-pinion steering systems prone to damage and failure. However, the more-robust recirculating-ball steering boxes on solid-axle steering are not free from failure, either.

Short of a major crash, such as a rollover, steering failures can quickly ruin a trip. Repairs can be difficult (assuming that spare parts are readily

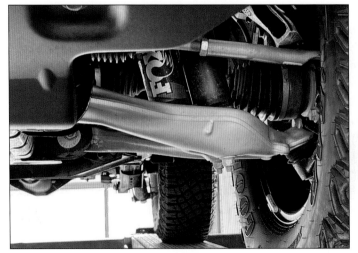

The steering geometry on the Bronco is spot on, but the cast materials used on the small-diameter tie-rods are just not up to the task of driving on rough and rutted off-road terrain.

available) and recoveries, such as towing, are extremely challenging. The most vulnerable components on all steering systems are stock tie-rods (and the tie-rod and drag link on solid-axle setups) and tie-rod ends. The tie-rods on rack-and-pinion steering systems are susceptible to failure due to the lightweight designs of the tie-rods and tie-rod ends. Solid-axle steering is more robust but only a little. For serious off-road adventures, especially on rough terrain, it is prudent to take advantage of the offerings by many aftermarket companies that make tie-rod and drag link upgrades. An alternative is to carry spare tie-rods and tie-rod ends.

Potential Problems

When a tie-rod becomes bent, toe settings usually change by a great amount to the point that steering is nearly impossible. The tie-rod weakens, so even if the rod can be straightened, it becomes more prone to further damage or failure. Damage and failures occur in bumpy, rutted terrain as well as in the rocks. Damage often occurs because a rut, rock, steep shelf obstacle, or bump is hit at too fast of a speed. In addition, the

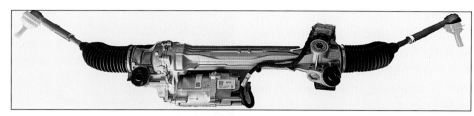

The stock Bronco steering system features an aluminum rack-and-pinion steering box with cast tie-rods. The system housing is sturdy, but the tie-rods are not. If a tie-rod fails, the support bushing at the end of the rack can become dislodged, causing more problems.

components are more vulnerable if the vehicle is also turning.

Tie-rod shafts can bend, and tie-rod ends can bend or break. Even minor damage where the toe alignment is thrown off can cause major issues with steering movement, even rendering the vehicle undrivable. Even being towed by another rig does not work (unless it's a tow truck that can lift the front end off the ground). While bent or broken tie-rods and tie-rod ends can occur on any vehicle, the lighter-weight components on independent front axle steering are much more vulnerable. When tie-rods fail, damage often occurs to the constant velocity (CV) joints as well.

Fortunately, several aftermarket companies offer strong components to reduce the risk of

failure. The aftermarket offers stronger steering components for nearly all overlanding-capable and rock-crawling vehicles.

The new Ford Bronco has perfect examples of issues with rack-and-pinion steering, even on new vehicles with few or no modifications. First, tie-rods and tie-rod ends are prone to bending and breaking under the heavy loads that are imposed by even moderate off-road terrain. The rack-and-pinion steering

Common Failure Points

All Steering Systems
- Steering gear wear
- Tie-rods
- Tie-rod ends
- Ball joints
- Steering arms
- Knuckles/spindles
- Steering-box mounting bolts

Unique to Rack-and-Pinion Steering
- Rack housing flex
- Rack bushing displacement (which renders the steering useless)
- Rack failure from major loads on rough terrain
- Front axle failure
- Tie-rod bending or failure
- Tie-rod end failure ■

When the front suspension goes into rebound travel (droops), the tie-rods run at an angle. If steering occurs in this situation while hitting a bump or rut, the tie-rods can fail.

box on the Bronco uses nylon-type bushings to support the toothed rack as it travels laterally. If the steering is turned full lock and heavy loads are encountered, the bushings can become dislodged, allowing the rack gear to disengage from the pinion gear, resulting in no steering.

Any style of steering system will experience wear, which leads to free play. Checking for free play is easy. If the steering wheel is turned in either direction by a few inches, the tires should also turn. If the steering-wheel movement is more than 1/8 to 1/4 inch total before the tires turn, the free play is probably excessive. In that case, all of the components should be checked, and the offending parts should be replaced.

Any off-road rig using stock steering components should carry spare tie-rods, tie-rod ends, and the tools to replace bent, broken, and damaged steering-system parts.

Aftermarket Upgrades

Nearly every off-road-capable vehicle enjoys good aftermarket product support specific to its brand. The availability of aftermarket steering upgrades for the Bronco has grown considerably since the launch of the new Bronco. Many companies offer upgraded steering components, especially tie-rods and tie-rod ends. Since any issue with steering creates a very difficult repair or vehicle recovery, upgrading steering components is important. If you upgrade tie-rods, it's wise to carry the old stock parts as spares just in case.

Tie-Rods

Upgraded tie-rods feature larger-diameter tubing with accommodations for larger tire-rod ends. The

Broncbuster makes a clamp to strengthen the stock Bronco tie-rods. The bracket clamps over the tie-rod. This is a good solution to strengthen the weak stock tie-rods.

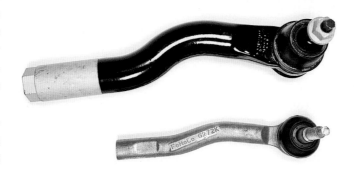

Tie-rod ends allow steering. Small-diameter shafts break while driving off-road. Aftermarket tie-rod ends provide much greater strength. Compare the stock Ford tie-rod end (bottom) to an aftermarket tie-rod end (top).

Racing at the King of the Hammers requires bulletproof parts. The massive tie-rod with a heavy-duty rod end is used to make sure that Loren Healy's 4500-class Bronco will not fail at the brutal event.

larger-diameter tubes with greater wall thickness increase strength dramatically. Stronger tie-rods greatly reduce the chance of damage or failure during the rigors of off-road driving. The stock tie-rods are even more prone to failure on lifted Broncos due to the angularity of the tie-rods. The

greater the lift, the worse the condition becomes. Some aftermarket tie-rods feature left- and right-hand threads for the tie-rod ends, allowing easy toe-setting adjustments without removing the outer tie-rod end from the steering knuckle. In addition to the complete tie-rod

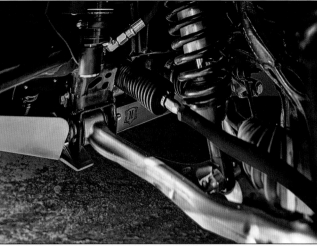

Icon Vehicle Dynamics produces a very stout replacement tie-rod system for the Bronco.

Superflex offers a tie-rod replacement package for the Bronco.

Foutz Motorsports manufactures two versions of its Bronco aftermarket tie-rods. Compare the Foutz tie-rods to the stock tie-rod at the top of the photo. The lower Foutz tie-rod is for the Bronco Raptor. (Photo Courtesy LiteBright Nation)

replacements, bolt-on sleeves covering and strengthening the factory tie-rod are also available.

Tie-Rod Ends

Factory tie-rod ends can break under the loads found on many off-road trails. If driving at too high of a speed, even easy trails have severe ruts and bumps that can cause damage and the breakage of vulnerable steering and suspension components. Aftermarket tie-rod ends greatly increase the strength of the assembly, reducing the risk of breakage on rough terrain. Some tie-rod upgrade kits include heavy-duty tie-rod ends, which increase strength and make toe adjustments simpler.

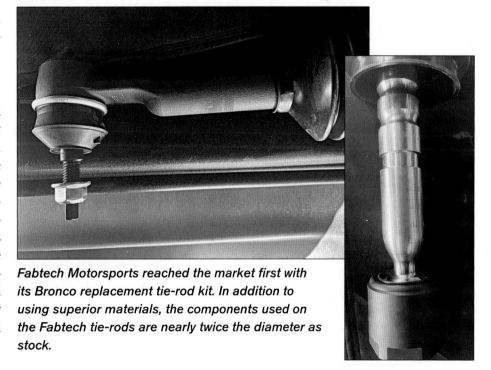

Fabtech Motorsports reached the market first with its Bronco replacement tie-rod kit. In addition to using superior materials, the components used on the Fabtech tie-rods are nearly twice the diameter as stock.

SteerSmarts offers very strong replacement tie-rod ends for the sixth-generation Bronco.

Steering Rack and Pinion

The steering rack consists of three basic components: 1) the rack housing, 2) the steering rack (a toothed bar that slides laterally to push/pull the tie-rods), and 3) a pinion gear that rotates as the steering wheel is turned to move the rack left and right. Stock steering-rack housings are generally fairly lightweight, usually made from cast aluminum. The housing tends to flex under heavy loads. This flex can cause the rack to bind internally, making steering difficult. The housing can also crack under more severe loads.

The toothed rack slides in bushings at each end of the housing as the steering is turned. On the Bronco, the heavy-duty plastic bushing can become displaced if a tie-rod bends or breaks. This eliminates steering, as the rack loses contact with the pinion gear.

BroncBuster offers a complete HOSS 3.0 steering rack upgrade package that provides greater steering power. The system includes beefy tie-rod braces. The system is a bolt-in replacement for the stock rack-and-pinion system. BroncBuster also offers a rack housing bushing replacement kit for the HOSS 3.0 system that eliminates the possibility of the rack sliding off the stock bush-

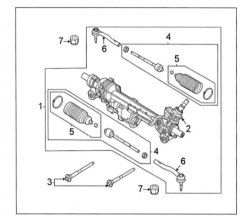

The HOSS 3.0 Bronco steering system features a strong rack-and-pinion steering box, but the end support bushing is prone to failure, especially if the small tie-rods fail.

Speedlogix offers billet-aluminum brackets that add considerable strength to the stock Bronco tie-rod.

The BroncBuster steering-rack housing bushings will not become dislodged if the tie-rods fail.

ings. Another BroncBuster kit is the ultimate steering upgrade package for the sixth-generation Ford Broncos. It includes the BroncBushing, the Buster Brace, and the all-new Stage III heavy-duty T6061 billet aluminum steering rack reinforcement housing. The housing has been designed to keep both sides of the steering rack and tie-rods from failing due to lifted steering geometry and extreme off-road forces.

Alignment

A good alignment shop can make a vehicle drive much better both on the highway and off-road. All four wheels need to be aligned. In addition to caster, camber, and toe-in, the rear axle must be centered in the chassis and square to the chassis. Modern alignment equipment makes this very accurate when using a well-equipped alignment or tire shop. A competent shop can also determine free play and the parts that need to be replaced.

Accurate suspension and steering alignment allow the vehicle to track

74Weld Rack Housing

74Weld manufactures a new steering-rack housing for the new Bronco. The 74Weld steering-rack housing is machined from billet aluminum. The housing uses the stock HOSS 2.0 and HOSS 3.0 internals to ensure that the electronics function properly. 74Weld redesigned how the rack bar is stabilized in the housing, eliminating the common failure points on both sides of the rack. The factory rack bar is stabilized by 1.5 points of contact. The 74Weld billet housing stabilizes the rack with four points of contact and adds a massive amount of material to high-stress housing areas, making it the strongest steering rack available.

This steering rack still maintains full OEM compatibility. The OEM rack is fully integrated with factory ABS electronics, and this critical component is fully maintained with the 74Weld billet Bronco steering rack. The internals and motor from a Ford Performance HOSS 3.0 rack is used to ensure proper electronic integration and compatibility with all OEM systems.

The 74Weld rack system will function perfectly for road driving with zero adverse effects. The fitment and feel are ideal for highway use, yet it's strong enough to take heavy off-road abuse. This rack has been tested throughout the country on some of the hardest trails by Loren Healy and the Fun-Haver crew. This is the rack that Healy runs in the FunRunner XL with 42s, long travel, and a 74Weld 4-gear race portals (see chapter 7). ■

The company 74Weld manufactures a new rack housing for the Bronco that is machined from billet aluminum. It has redesigned how the rack bar is stabilized in the housing, eliminating the common failure points on both sides of the rack. The factory rack bar is stabilized by 1.5 points of contact. The 74Weld housing stabilizes the rack with four points of contact and adds a massive amount of material to high-stress housing areas, making it the strongest steering rack available.

The 74Weld billet Bronco steering rack maintains full OEM compatibility. The OEM rack is fully integrated with factory antilock braking system (ABS) electronics, and this critical component is fully maintained with the 74Weld steering rack. The internals and motor from a Ford Performance HOSS 3.0 rack is used to ensure proper electronic integration and compatibility with all OEM systems. The fitment and feel of the 74Weld rack system are ideal for highway use, yet strong enough to take heavy off-road abuse. This rack has been tested throughout the country on some of the hardest trails by Loren Healy and the Fun-Haver Off-Road crew.

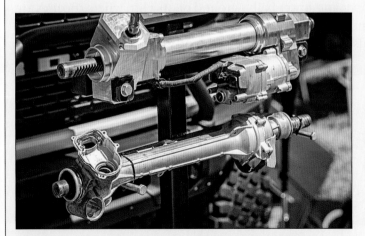

This is the steering rack Loren Healey runs in the Fun-Runner XL with 42s, long travel, and 74Weld four-gear race portals (see chapter 7).

The Fun-Haver Off-Road race-prepped Bronco driven by Loren Healy dominated the 4500 class at the 2023 King of the Hammers race in Johnson Valley, California.

straight and provide good stability. When the suspension and steering are out of alignment, the steering can pull in one direction. Tire scrub will increase tire wear, reduce fuel economy, and even negatively impact vehicle stability.

Suspension Control Arms and Steering Linkages

Most stock steering and suspension linkages have a single tie-rod end that is threaded into the bar for adjustment. The rod end is secured into place with a jam nut. The jam nut must be loosened before the rod end or tie-rod end is removed from its mounting location. Then, the rod end or tie-rod end can be rotated in or out to adjust the arm length for the correct alignment. The rod end or tie-rod end is then reinstalled. Finally, the jam nut is tightened.

Many aftermarket suspension kits and steering linkages have rod ends or tie-rod ends at each end of the link. These ends are threaded, with one end a standard right-hand thread and the other end a left-hand thread. This allows the tube or linkage to be rotated after each jam nut is loosened without removing either the tie-rod or rod ends from the mounting location. This makes the alignment process much easier, quicker and more accurate.

Alignment Tools

Common tools are needed for alignment, including a tape measure and a digital magnetic level for adjusting caster and pinion angles. Large wrenches are necessary to tighten the jam nuts after the control arms, track bars, drag link, and tie-rods are adjusted to the correct lengths. A helper to hold the other end of the tape measure makes sus-pension alignment much easier and more accurate.

Aligning the Rear Axle Housings

Measure to determine that the axle is perpendicular to the frame. In other words, you should have the exact same distance from the reference point that you selected on the left and right frame rails to the same spot on the left and right of the axle. You can pick either lower control arm to adjust this. Adjust one longer or adjust the other shorter. Now, your axle is straight, or "square" in the frame, and you'll go straight down the road.

Once this task is complete for the rear axle and the wheels and tires have been fitted, set the vehicle on the ground. Next, adjust the rear track bar to get the rig sitting centered left to right, side to side. Locate identical places on the frame on both sides and measure horizontally to something fixed on the axle or wheel to get the same distance on the left side as the right side. Centering the axle side to side under the frame is the goal.

Setting Front Axle Caster

Caster is the angle of a line passing through the upper and lower ball joint centers. You need the magnetic level to measure this angle. Use man-ufacturer specifications on independent front suspension systems.

First, set the level on the ground directly below the lower ball joint in the steering knuckle. Zero the magnetic level on the ground. Place the level on the flat spot at the bottom of the knuckle. The difference in the angle from the ground to the angle on the bottom of the spindle is the positive caster angle (the top of the spindle is tilted toward the rear of the vehicle). Adjust the eccentric bushings to achieve the optimal desired caster angle. Tighten the nut.

Setting Front Axle Toe

Adjust the tie-rod lengths to the manufacturers toe-in specifications. Make adjustments while the vehicle is on the ground with the front tires pointing straight ahead. Left- and right-side tires should have the exact same toe settings. Each tie-rod should be adjusted to the same length.

Setting Rear Axle Pinion Angle

The pinion angle is adjusted with the rear suspension control arms the same way that axle squareness is set. Angles should be measured with the vehicle at ride height (either on level ground or on a lift, where the tires are on ramps with the weight of vehicle resting on the tires). Either upper or

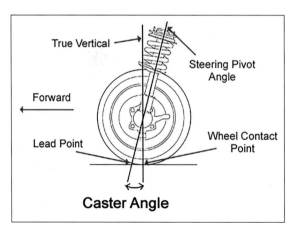

Caster Angle

Caster is the tilt of the steering axis on the front independent suspension. Caster helps road feel of the steering and affects the return to center of the steering as the steering wheel is turned back to center by the driver. Each Bronco model has slightly different caster settings, but all are in the range of 3.2 to 3.6 degrees positive caster.

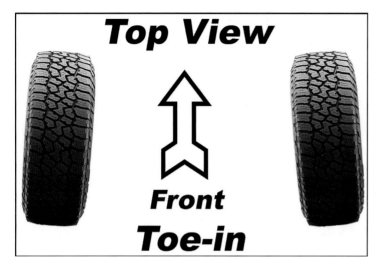

Top View

Front

Toe-in

Toe-in on the front suspension is the angle of the front tires compared to straight (90 degrees from the centerline of the vehicle). Toe-in is present when the front edges of the tires are angled toward each other, while toe-out occurs if the tires angle away from each other. On an independent front suspension vehicle, each side of the front end must be aligned separately, but each side should be set to the same toe-in setting. A solid-axle front suspension has only one tie-rod, so only one adjustment is needed. Refer to the shop manual for exact toe setting as each model varies slightly.

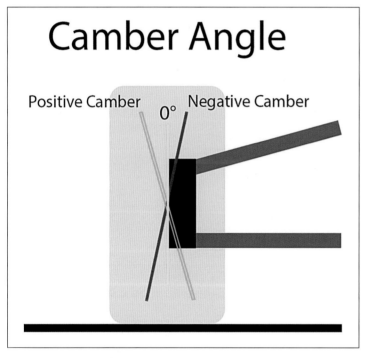

Camber Angle

Positive Camber   0°   Negative Camber

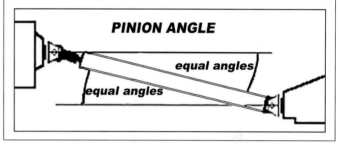

PINION ANGLE

equal angles

equal angles

The pinion angle is the angle of the rear driveshaft at the front on the transfer case and at the rear on the rear axle pinion shaft. The two angles should be equal (as the diagram shows).

Camber is the tilt of the tire from vertical when viewed from the front of the vehicle. Positive camber exists when the top of tire tilts toward the outside of the vehicle. Zero camber occurs when the tire is truly vertical. Negative camber means that the top of the tire tilts toward the middle of the vehicle.

lower rear control arms can be used to adjust pinion angle.

Using the upper versus the lower depends on how much thread is available for adjustment. One control arm (either upper or lower—depending on which is used for adjustment) should be disconnected from the axle housing while the opposite arm is adjusted. Then, the disconnected arm is adjusted so that it easily slides into the bracket. In other words, the left- and right-side control arm should be equal length.

The correct pinion angle depends on the angle of the engine, transmission, and transfer case, which is almost always pointing downhill at the rear of the engine, etc. The engine crankshaft, transmission shafts, and transfer shafts are all perfectly parallel with each other. The pinion shaft should be parallel to the engine crankshaft, etc.

The angle of the engine at the rear should be in the 1- to 3-degree range down at the back. The angle measurement can be taken from any perpendicular surface on the back of the transfer case or the front of the engine, such as the crankshaft vibration damper. The suspension control arms are adjusted to rotate the axle housing and pinion shaft to the same angle, with the pinion shaft pointing uphill at the front of the housing. Angles should be within a half degree of each other to eliminate driveshaft vibrations.

*B*RAKES

The sixth-generation Bronco features large brakes (front and rear) on all trim levels. When Jeep launched the Wrangler JL and Gladiator, the brake packages were larger than the previous Wrangler JK.

Even though Jeep stepped up its game with the brakes on the Jeep Wrangler JL and Gladiator, the Bronco uses even larger brakes on all models. The Bronco uses larger brake rotors and calipers with larger-diameter pistons. See the "Stock Wrangler and Bronco Brake Comparison" table for details.

Steep descents require good brake performance even with four-wheel-drive low range and first gear. The brake system needs to be capable of controlling downhill speed without excessive pedal pressure from the driver. The Bronco's 1-Pedal Drive and Hill Assist features work quite well. Brake upgrades help when using tires over 37 inches in diameter.

Stock Wrangler and Bronco Brake Comparison		
	Wrangler JL	**Sixth-Generation Bronco**
Type	Power-assisted, anti-lock braking system	Four-wheel power disc brakes with four-sensor, four-channel antilock braking system and electronic stability control; boost: 2.3L engine (vacuum brake boost), 2.7L engine (electronic brake boost)
Front Rotor Size and Type	12.9 x 0.94 (330 x 24) vented rotor (Sport)	Vented discs, twin-piston floating caliper
	12.9 x 1.1 (330 x 28) vented rotor (Sahara and Rubicon)	350 x 34 mm
Front Caliper Size and Type	1.88 (48) twin-piston floating caliper (Sport)	Vented discs, twin-piston floating caliper
	2 (51) twin-piston floating caliper (Sahara and Rubicon)	2 x 51 mm
Rear Rotor Size and Type	2.9 x 0.47 (328 x 12) solid rotor (Sport)	Rotor diameter/thickness 311 mm x 34 mm
	13.4 x 0.55 (342 x 14) solid rotor (Sahara and Rubicon)	—
Rear Caliper Size and Type	1.77 (45) single-piston floating caliper (Sport)	Discs with single-piston floating caliper, integral electronic parking brake
	1.88 (48) single-piston floating caliper (Sahara and Rubicon)	1 x 54 mm

The factory brakes on the Bronco Wildtrak and other Bronco models provide plenty of stopping power for steep descents with the original 35-inch-diameter tires.

The larger rotors and dual-piston floating front calipers on the Bronco provide excellent braking performance. While brake upgrades are always a good idea, the Bronco does not really need brake upgrades with tires that are up to 37 inches in diameter. Since 40-inch tires are becoming more common, brake upgrades should be considered or even planned for that situation. Consider upgrading rotors and pads when wear requires replacement of the stock rotors and pads.

Brake Specifications	
Front type	Power antilock front disc
Booster type	Electronically controlled brake boost
Front rotor diameter/thickness/material	350 mm x 34 mm Nitro Tough Iron
Front caliper configuration	2 x 51 mm sliding caliper
Front pad material	FER9213
Front swept area	79.9 square inches
Rear type	Power antilock front disc
Rear rotor diameter/thickness/material	336 mm x 20 mm Nitro Tough Iron
Rear caliper configuration	1 x 54 mm sliding electronic integrated parking brake (EIPB)
Rear pad material	GA9105
Rear swept area	63.5 square inches
Parking/emergency brake	25.5 kN electronic parking brake

Dual-piston calipers provide improved stopping performance by distributing the braking force over a larger area of the brake pad. The front calipers on the Bronco are a two-piston design, allowing great braking performance from the stock brakes.

The piston on the single-piston rear caliper on the Bronco is larger than on most similar vehicles. This allows the use of larger brake pads on the large 13-inch-diameter rotor.

The rear brakes on the sixth-generation Broncos use a floating single-piston caliper, providing more-than-adequate stopping power. The rotor diameter on the Bronco is larger than on most other similar vehicles.

The front rotors on the Bronco measure 13.75 inches in diameter with a thickness of 1.34 inches. The rotors are very thick and the large diameter increases stopping power by providing more leverage.

Braking Elements

Larger tires weigh more than smaller tires, and much of the additional weight that is added to larger tires is added to the tire tread. Weight farther from the center of rotation adds to the rotational inertia effect. When weight is rotated, it takes force to begin and cease the rotation. If the weight is closer to the center of rotation, less force is needed to begin the rotation. If weight is moved away from the center of rotation, it takes more force to move the weight. More force is also needed to slow and stop the rotation. Think of a flywheel. A lightweight, small-diameter flywheel allows an engine to rev quickly and easily. The lightweight flywheel also loses revs very quickly. If the lightweight, small flywheel is replaced with a heavy, large-diameter one, the engine will rev more slowly and also take longer to reduce RPM. Big tires act the same way. The Bronco offers large enough rotors and a large enough brake pad area that handling larger tires is within the capability of the stock brakes.

Steep descents even on dirt require powerful brakes. The large brakes on the Bronco with the dual-piston front caliper allow gentle brake applications without locking the brakes. When descending a steep, loose dirt hill, it is easy to lock up the rear brakes, even with an antilock braking system. Locking the rear brakes while turning can cause the rear tires to slide sideways, creating a situation where the vehicle can roll over.

Larger tires, such as the 37-inch-diameter Nitto tires on Kevin and Brittany Williams's Bronco Raptor, require big brakes for optimal stopping power. The good news for sixth-generation Bronco owners is that the original equipment brakes provide good stopping power, even with 37-inch tires.

Stopping distances do not increase very much when stepping up to 37-inch tires (when compared to the 35-inch-diameter tires on the Sasquatch package–equipped Broncos). Stopping at maximum rates of deceleration (panic stops) do require more brake pedal pressure. Increasing the tire size to 40-inch diameter will affect stopping distances as well, requiring even more brake-pedal pressure. Brake rotors and pads will heat more and wear faster. On challenging trails off-road, the negative effects of larger tires is even more pronounced.

Can the brakes apply enough force to control speed when dropping down a steep ledge? The stock Bronco brakes will stop tire rotation on smaller vertical drop offs with the OEM tires. More brake pedal pressure is needed with larger-diameter tires to lock the tires up on steep drops. Larger-diameter rotors, softer brake pads, and calipers with additional clamping force can all contribute to improved performance.

If the tires can be locked up by the brakes on a drop off, it is up to the tires to provide adequate traction to control the descent speed of the vehicle. If the brake system cannot develop adequate clamping force (the force pressing the brake pads against the rotors through the pistons), the vehicle will drop off a ledge too quickly, causing more impact that is desirable when the tires drop down. While locking up tires is not desirable to keep drop-off speeds low, the ability to do so is important. If the tires stop rolling too easily, then the tire traction is the issue. Either the tires do not offer enough traction or the tire pressure is too high.

The vented original equipment replacement rotors for the Bronco are adequate for tires up to 37 inches in diameter. Upgrading to aftermarket drilled and/or slotted rotors will improve braking performance on extreme terrain with larger off-road tires.

Rotors

Brake rotors are the heart of the braking system. With clamping force from the brake pads, the rotors reduce the rotation of the wheel and tire. The friction needed to accomplish this important job generates considerable heat. Brake rotors come in two styles: vented and solid. Vented rotors help dissipate heat for better braking performance in extreme conditions. The Bronco comes from the factory with large front vented brake rotors. Most aftermarket rotors are drilled or slotted (sometimes both). This helps dissipate heat and allows the gases created by brake-pad degradation to escape more easily.

A simple way to improve brake performance requires upgrading brake rotors. PowerStop offers several brake rotor upgrades, ranging from stock-replacement rotors to extreme-duty rotors for off-road performance and towing. PowerStop provides options for drilled, slotted, and coated rotors. Drilled and slotted rotors help to evacuate the gases emitted by the heating of friction material on the brake pads. Coated rotors help dissipate heat and improve wear characteristics. EBC, Wilwood, APD, Brembo, and Raybestos (among others) offer rotors and brake pads for the Bronco.

Calipers

Brake calipers turn hydraulic pressure from the master cylinder through the brake lines into clamping force. The clamping force squeezes the brake pads against the brake rotor. Brake calipers have pistons internally activated by the brake pedal. The pistons push the

For exceptional brake performance improvements, rigid-design calipers with pistons on each side of the caliper provide improved stopping power. Wilwood offers complete packages.

pads against the rotors to provide stopping power. Floating calipers have one or two pistons on one side of the caliper. The other side of the caliper "floats" to squeeze the pads against the rotor. Two piston calipers can generate more clamping force. Rigid calipers feature pistons on each side of the caliper with two or three pistons per side. Rigid calipers can generate more clamping force. Larger calipers allow the use of larger brake pads. More brake pad area translates into more braking force for a given pedal pressure. The Bronco features two-piston floating calipers on the front and single-piston floating calipers on the rear.

Stock-replacement calipers are available from several companies. Stock replacements do little to improve stock braking performance. To gain significant braking performance improvements, a complete brake kit, including rotors, calipers, and brake pads is needed.

Pads

Brake pads consist of a friction material that creates stopping power when pressed against the brake rotors by the calipers. Brake pads are available in different hardness compounds. Brake pads need heat to most effectively create stopping friction. Softer compounds generate heat more quickly, while harder compounds take longer to create heat.

Most original equipment brake pads are on the soft side to allow quick heat build-up, especially for emergency stopping situations. Harder compounds are used in extreme conditions, such as towing heavy loads or driving on curvy mountain roads where hard braking occurs constantly. For off-road

Many companies offer aftermarket brake pads. For normal highway and off-road driving, a soft pad compound improves braking performance at highway speeds. On the trail, the soft-compound pads generate maximum deceleration power quickly, unlike hard-compound brake pads. At low speeds on the trail, especially when climbing rocks and dropping off steep ledges, the soft-compound pads will generate brake force almost instantly.

driving, while brake performance is critical in extreme rock crawling and steep hill descents, speeds are very low. Maximum braking force is necessary at low speed, requiring a soft brake-pad compound. OEM brake pads do a good job off-road.

While several companies offer replacement brake pads in a variety of compounds, most companies offer

brake pad and rotor packages so that the rotor materials and the brake-pad compounds are compatible for optimal performance and wear.

Kits

Each element of the braking system must be compatible with the other parts. Upgrading the brake

For optimal braking performance upgrades, install a complete brake kit, including rotors, calipers, pads, hats, and hardware. It's a big investment, but in extreme conditions and in competition, the cost is worthwhile.

system with a complete kit ensures that the brakes will function as desired. Bear, Wilwood, Brembo, and Alcon offer complete kits, including rotors, calipers, pads, and hardware. Several companies offer rotor and brake pad upgrades that work with the stock calipers. While this minimal upgrade helps improve braking performance, the increase is much less than offered by complete kits. Kits including calipers use larger-diameter rotors and larger brake pads. The increased brake-pad surface area provides more stopping power. The calipers in the complete kits generally have more piston area and provide greater clamping force, which makes brake pedal effort more manageable with larger-diameter tires.

Most complete kits use rigid calipers with four to six pistons. The rigid caliper design with pistons on both sides of the caliper provide greater clamping force than the same area of a piston on a floating caliper.

Fluid

Brake fluid is hygroscopic, which means that the fluid absorbs water vapor from the air. For this reason, use small pint containers of brake fluid and keep them sealed tightly when not pouring fluid into the master-cylinder reservoir. Water vapor in the fluid will lower the boiling point of the fluid. This increases compressibility and can cause a spongy brake pedal—or even no pedal. Clearly, this can be dangerous. Once contaminated the brake fluid must be purged from the system and replaced with fresh fluid.

The Department of Transportation specifies three common types of brake fluid: DOT 3, DOT 4, and DOT 5. DOT 3 and 4 are the preferred types for high-performance, high-temperature use and are available in a wide range of formulations and performance characteristics. DOT 3 fluids are usually less expensive than DOT 4 fluids and are not

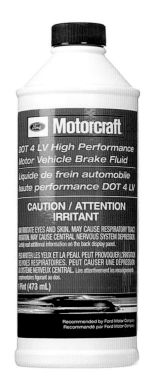

Ford recommends Motorcraft DOT 4 LV High Performance Motor Vehicle Brake Fluid for the sixth-generation Bronco.

as capable in extreme use. DOT 5 is a silicon-based fluid (rather than glycol-based), which is not good for high-temperature use because it expands, becomes compressible, and makes the pedal soft and spongy.

Brake Pad and Rotor Break-In *Text Courtesy Wilwood Brakes*

The following is a typical example of brake pad break-in procedures.

Once the brake system has been tested and determined to be safe to use to operate the vehicle, follow these steps for the bedding of all new pad materials. These procedures should only be performed on a racetrack or other safe location, where you can safely and legally obtain speeds up to 65 mph while also being able to rapidly decelerate.

Begin with a series of light decelerations to gradually build some heat in the brakes. Use an on-and-off the pedal technique by applying the brakes for 3 to 5 seconds, and then allow them to fully release for a period roughly twice as long as the deceleration cycle. If you use a 5 count during the deceleration interval, use a 10 count during the release to allow the heat to sink into the pads and rotors.

After several cycles of light stops to begin warming the brakes, proceed with a series of medium to firm deceleration stops to continue raising the temperature level in the brakes.

Finish the bedding cycle with a series of 8 to 10 hard decelerations from 55 to 65 mph down to 25 mph while allowing a proportionate release and heat-sinking interval between each stop. The pads should now be providing positive and consistent response.

If any amount of brake fade is observed during the bed-in cycle, immediately begin the cool down cycle.

Drive at a moderate cruising speed, with the least amount of brake contact possible, until most of the heat has dissipated from the brakes. Avoid sitting stopped with the brake pedal depressed to hold the car in place during this time. Park the vehicle and allow the brakes to cool to ambient air temperature.

It should be noted that other brake manufacturers use slightly different procedures. It is important to follow the recommended procedures to optimize brake-system performance and life. ∎

DRIVELINE

The driveline on the sixth-generation Broncos provides excellent options for off-road performance. That's the good news! For most off-road driving situations, the Bronco's driveline durability is good. For extreme off-roading, the bad news is that there is a lack of driveline durability, especially for rock crawling on larger off-road tires.

This is no different from other vehicles. Even the axle assemblies on the solid-axle Jeep Wranglers suffer from failures in extreme conditions.

The Bronco's front axle shafts (half shafts) and CV joints are prone to failure in extreme conditions, especially when the driver lacks throttle finesse. In addition, the independent front suspension contributes to the lack of durability. The problem is exacerbated when suspension lifts exceed 2 inches where axle shaft angles are more severe. The aftermarket offers excellent upgrades to help improve durability and performance.

Ford hit a home run with the gearing options for the Bronco on the transmission and axle ratios. Combined with great engine torque, the off-road and highway performance is exceptional, especially with the Bronco Raptor. Crawl ratios provide excellent climbing and descending ability with any tire combination up to 38 inches in diameter. Large 40-inch (or taller) tires benefit from lower gearing and beefier driveline components.

Axle lockers come standard on the Badlands and Wildtrak (rear only) models and with any model equipped with the Sasquatch package. The electric lockers perform quite well in poor-traction situations. The lockers on the Bronco are actually lockers—not computer-controlled versions that cut power to the wheel with excessive wheelspin. Air lockers, E-lockers, and limited-slip rear differentials are offered by the aftermarket. Rear driveshafts offering improved strength are also available from the aftermarket.

Broncos, especially those equipped with the Sasquatch package, offer great off-road performance. The Wildtrak model is good in the rocks but better in the desert environment. Front drive (half) shafts are prone to accelerate wear and possible failure under the heavier loads of rock crawling, especially with a suspension lift that exceeds 2 inches. Curiously, the Wildtrak model comes with a single rear locker.

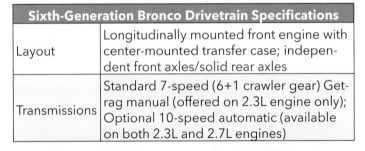

The Bronco front axle (half) shafts provide good strength for most off-road situations. The shafts are fairly short, so excessive angularity puts heavy stress on the constant velocity (CV) joints. Any suspension lift increases the axle shaft angles, which increases the load on the CV joints and accelerates wear.

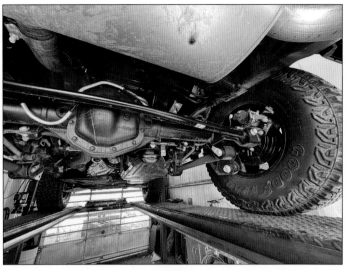

The rear axle housing on the Bronco is fairly stout, but like any solid axle housing used for higher-speed desert driving or rock crawling, using a stronger housing is a good idea. Weld-on trusses can increase strength considerably.

Sixth-Generation Bronco Drivetrain Specifications	
Layout	Longitudinally mounted front engine with center-mounted transfer case; independent front axles/solid rear axles
Transmissions	Standard 7-speed (6+1 crawler gear) Getrag manual (offered on 2.3L engine only); Optional 10-speed automatic (available on both 2.3L and 2.7L engines)

Gear Ratios		
Gear	7-Speed Manual	10-Speed Automatic
Crawler	6.588:1	N/A
First	4.283:1	4.714:1
Second	2.365:1	2.997:1
Third	1.453:1	2.149:1
Fourth	1.000:1	1.769:1
Fifth	0.776:1	1.521:1
Sixth	0.646:1	1.275:1
Seventh	N/A	1.000:1
Eighth	N/A	0.853:1
Ninth	N/A	0.689:1
Tenth	N/A	0.636:1
Reverse	-5.625:1	-4.885:1

Transfer Cases	
Standard	• 4x4 with part-time engagement electronic shift on the fly (ESOF) • 2.72:1 low ratio
Optional	• Advanced 4x4 with 4A mode automatic on-demand engagement • 3.06:1 low ratio
Crawl Ratios	*Maximum* • 79.92:1 (7-speed manual with standard ESOF) • 57.19:1 (10-speed speed automatic with standard ESOF) *Optional* • 94.75:1 (7-speed manual with optional Advanced 4x4) • 67.80:1 (10-speed automatic with optional Advanced 4x4)
Axles	• Front standard Dana AdvanTEK M190 independent front suspension • Rear Dana 44 AdvanTEK M220 solid rear differential • Optional front Dana AdvanTEK M210 independent front suspension with Spicer Performa-TraK electronic locker • Rear Dana 44 AdvanTEK M220 solid rear differential with Spicer Performa-TraK electronic locker

Available Final-Drive Ratios			
Model	Manual	Automatic	Sasquatch
Base	4.46:1	3.73:1	4.70:1
Big Bend	4.46:1	3.73:1/4.27:1	4.70:1
Black Diamond	4.46:1	4.46:1	4.70:1
Outer Banks	N/A	3.73:1/4.27:1	4.70:1
Wildtrak	N/A	4.46:1	4.70:1
First Edition	N/A	N/A	4.70:1
• Aftermarket sixth-generation Bronco axle ratios: 4.88, 5.13, and 5.38			
• Ford uses ratios not compatible with Ford 9-inch and Dana			

One of the challenges when choosing gear ratios for an off-road vehicle is the compromise in gearing for the highway and for off-road driving, On the highway, the first consideration is the final drive ratio, which determines the speed of the vehicle at a given engine RPM. A numerically higher ratio means that the vehicle will travel at a slower speed for a given engine RPM (all else being equal).

The second important detail relates to off-road performance in low range in the transfer case. The crawl ratio is a measure of the final gear ratio in low range in the transfer case and first gear in the transmission. The crawl ratio is determined by multiplying the axle ratio by the transmission ratio and then multiplying the result by the transfer-case ratio.

A Bronco with a Sasquatch package with an automatic transmission in first gear and low range has a crawl ratio of 67.8 with the Advanced 4x4 option (the manual-transmission version has a whopping 94.75 crawl ratio). The higher the numerical crawl ratio number, the slower the vehicle speed at a given engine RPM. The higher number also translates into more torque multiplication, which is important when climbing hills and rock crawling. The higher crawl ratio number also helps keep speeds lower when descending steep hills.

Ring-and-Pinion Gear Upgrades

The sixth-generation Bronco offers several axle ratio gearing options. The Badlands and Sasquatch packages use the 4.71 ring-and-pinion ratio. Combined with the substantial torque output and the very favorable crawl ratio, upgrading the ring and pinion to a lower ratio (higher numerically) is not really necessary unless the tire diameter exceeds 38 inches. Several aftermarket companies offer ring and pinons in alternated ratios, but most only offer gearsets for the rear axle. Aftermarket

The Bronco with a Sasquatch package with an automatic transmission in first gear and low range has a crawl ratio of 67.8, which is outstanding, especially considering the high torque output of the engine. The manual-transmission version has a whopping 94.75 crawl ratio, which is likely better than any stock 4x4 currently available.

Ford uses unusual axle ratios in the Bronco. Several companies offer ring-and-pinion gearsets for the Bronco rear and front differentials, which have a different structure compared to the more common Dana and Ford 9-inch differentials.

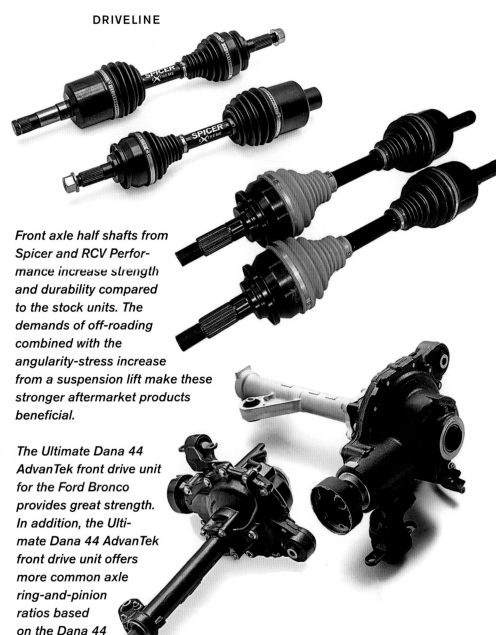

companies include Yukon Gear & Axle, Alloy USA, Revolution, Motive Gear, and Dana Spicer.

Axle Upgrades

Axle shafts are a weak link in the driveline. This includes the front axle shafts or half shafts. Axle shafts can twist or break. The most common cause of axle shaft issues relates to wheelspin. When a driver applies too much throttle in slippery conditions (especially on rocks), wheelspin occurs.

The spinning tires heat up, which allows the tires to generate more traction and possibly wear through moisture or loose sand and dirt. A sudden increase in traction can cause an axle shaft to break (or a rear driveshaft to twist). Larger tires on stock axles increase the chance of axle breakage. Stock axle shafts are generally made from 1040 or 1541 steel. Aftermarket rear axle shafts for the Bronco are often made from 4340 chromoly steel and heat treated. Chromoly shafts are much more durable and less prone to breaking.

Front Axle Shafts (Half Shafts)

Extreme-duty front-axle half shafts are available from Spicer and RCV Performance. These axles provide much greater strength compared to the stock Bronco shafts. The Spicer and RCV half shafts are very pricey. The stock differential and housing are retained, but the stock components are not very durable for extreme off-roading. The ultimate solution for improved performance and durability is the Ultimate Dana 44 AdvanTEK front drive unit, which provides significantly increased strength and durability for the Ford Bronco for off-road performance.

Front axle half shafts from Spicer and RCV Performance increase strength and durability compared to the stock units. The demands of off-roading combined with the angularity-stress increase from a suspension lift make these stronger aftermarket products beneficial.

The Ultimate Dana 44 AdvanTek front drive unit for the Ford Bronco provides great strength. In addition, the Ultimate Dana 44 AdvanTek front drive unit offers more common axle ring-and-pinion ratios based on the Dana 44 architecture.

Ultimate Dana 44 AdvanTEK Front Drive Unit Axle Features and Benefits

- The Dana-designed, cast-iron center housing allows for deep gear ratios not supported by the factory front drive unit.
- The 32-spline differential side gears provide improved strength for better off-road performance.
- The electronic locking differential offers optimal traction when you need it.
- It allows the choice of the best gear ratio for your sixth-generation Ford Bronco.
- It comes fully loaded and ready to install to save time and money.
- The cast-iron tube provides added strength over the stock aluminum tube. ∎

With a 32-spline differential and an aftermarket-exclusive housing that allows you to use your choice of gear ratio, the Ultimate 44 AdvanTEK front drive unit is ready to install right out of the crate.

The greatest advantage when using the stronger front axle shafts is improved strength. When a Bronco is lifted, the angle of the front axle shafts changes. This places additional stress on the CV joints. The recommend maximum lift on independent front suspicion rigs is 2 inches. Even the increased angle on the axles with a 2-inch lift accelerates wear and increases the possibility of CV joint failure. Lifts more than 2 inches exacerbate the situation. Front axle half shafts from Spicer or RCV Performance reduce the risk of failure substantially.

Rear Axles and Axle Assemblies

Axle upgrades for the Bronco rear axle are available from several suppliers. The axle housing can also be trussed to increase rigidity. Stronger axles and axle housings improve reliability, but axle gear ratio selections are limited. The latest solution for extreme off-road situations comes from Dana. The Ultimate Dana 60

The Ultimate Dana 60 rear axle assembly design allows an easy bolt-in installation. As with the Ultimate Dana 44 AdvanTek front drive unit, the Dana Ultimate 60 rear axle uses the more common Dana ring-and-pinion ratios.

TECH TIP

Ultimate Dana 60 Semi-Float Axle Features and Benefits

- Double-row, tapered-roller axle bearings deliver crucial strength and weight capability.
- High-strength 35-spline chromoly axle shafts are used for durability.
- There is an electronic or air locking differential option.
- Choose the best gear ratio for your sixth-generation Ford Bronco.

rear axle assembly offers improved performance, better gear-ratio selections and enhanced strength.

The Ultimate Dana 60 is a bolt-on replacement, featuring Spicer chromoly steel axle shafts, Spicer

The Spidertrax rear axle assembly is based on the Ford 9-inch housing. The Spidertrax assembly is the strongest available and used by many of the King of the Hammers competitors, including Loren Healey in the Fun-Haver Off-Road Ford Bronco.

ring-and-pinion gearing, heavy-duty brackets, a Dana nodular-iron differential cover, and more.

The major caveat when using the Ultimate Dana 60 rear axle assembly is the need to also use the Ultimate Dana 44 AdvanTEK front drive unit. This is necessary for gear-ratio compatibility. The Dana Ultimate axle assemblies use gears found in other Dana axles. The ratios are not compatible with the OEM Ford ratios found in the Bronco.

Selectable Axle Lockers

Differential (axle) lockers physically lock the left- and right-side axles together so that the axles rotate at the same speed. Differentials are designed so that one wheel on an axle can freewheel. While cornering, the inside tire will rotate slower than the outside tire. The differential allows this to occur without tire scrub. A differential locker locks the left- and right-side wheels together. This increases traction but also increases tire scrub and steering effort when cornering. Differential lockers are usually associated with extreme four wheeling situations. However, if you drive in sand, mud, snow, or ice, having at least one differential locker makes life much easier in adverse conditions. Selectable lockers allow the driver to select when the locker engages by using a switch that activates a solenoid, which engages the locker with an electrified magnet or compressed air.

Some new Broncos come equipped with electric lockers on both the front and rear axles. While electric lockers work quite well, they are prone to failure in extreme conditions, often due to electrical issues and actuator failure. Aftermarket E-Lockers tend to be more durable and are a good choice if you are upgrading on models with no lockers. Air lockers use compressed air from a compressor (or a compressed-gas source, such as the CO_2 in a Power Tank). Air lockers are more durable and activate more quickly.

Portal Axles

Portal axles consist of a gearset that attaches to the hub assembly. This lifts the chassis without affecting the suspension geometry, which is very beneficial for an independent front suspension rig. The internal gears within the portal-axle assembly can be configured to alter the gear ratio, which may mean

that it is unnecessary to re-gear the ring-and-pinion gears to accommodate larger, taller tires.

Portal axles were somewhat popular a few decades ago on Land Rovers. Recently, portal axles have found favor in extreme off-road events, such as King of the Hammers.

Now, portals are finding their way into more extreme Bronco builds. 74Weld, which was mentioned in the steering chapter (it makes a beautiful billet aluminum steering rack housing for the Bronco), also manufactures portal axles for the Bronco. The portal axles lift the chassis by 4 inches. That means that no lift is needed for the suspension to create clearance for taller tires.

An added benefit (maybe even more important) is the suspension geometry remaining stock. Stock compression and rebound travel remains unaltered unlike using a spring lift. Spring lifts increase up travel while reducing down travel. This makes it easier to lift tires off the ground during articulation.

Bronco 74Weld 4-Gear Portal Axle Kit Features

- It was designed for Broncos equipped with single shear steering.
- There is a 22-percent reduction at the hub allows for use of larger 37- to 39-inch tires.
- It does not require re-gearing of your axles.
- The Portal system acts as a lift and a re-gear.
- It maintains suspension geometry while increasing ground clearance.
- It features billet aluminum construction with premium steel inserts.
- It is factory ABS compatible.
- It is a direct bolt-on design.

The 74Weld portal axles also include a 1.22 to 1 ratio, which increases the crawl ratio. The 4.70:1 axle ratio found on Sasquatch packages would effectively become a 5.73:1 ratio, a vast improvement for running taller, heavier tires.

Photos do not do justice to the engineering and manufacturing of the 74Weld portal axles. They are truly works of art.

Portal axles from 74Weld played a key role in the total dominance of the Fun-Haver Off-Road Ford Bronco at the 2024 King of the Hammers event. Loren Healey drove the 4600 stock-class Bronco to victory. The buggy version, also driven by Loren Healey, nearly won the 4400 classes the following day. A minor parts failure stopped Healey about a mile from the finish line of the grueling event. (Photo Courtesy Ford Motor Company/Fun-Haver Off-Road)

ENGINE AND TRANSMISSION UPGRADES

Ford did a masterful job executing the engine and transmission package on the sixth-generation Bronco lineup, except a V-8 would have been awesome and true to the Bronco heritage. While rumors of Ford offering a V-8 option for the Bronco appear, the rumors were most likely wishful thinking. Don't hold your breath.

Engine Upgrades

The bottom line for Bronco engine upgrades is that they are not really necessary. The torque of the stock engine provides excellent performance. Since the V-6 engines are turbocharged, there's no need for adding forced induction. Speaking of turbos, the Bronco shows some turbo lag. Most modern turbocharged vehicles have virtually eliminated turbo lag.

The first time I drove a turbocharged race car (a front wheel-drive sedan) I was completely caught off-guard by the turbo lag. During a test session (after a warm-up), I was exiting the last turn onto the main straight. As always, I fed more power as I exited the turn. Suddenly, the boost hit, adding about 75 hp. The front tires protested, causing wheelspin

The Ford 2.7L EcoBoost engine offers 330 hp with premium fuel, 315 hp with regular fuel, a whopping 415 ft-lbs of torque, and decent fuel economy (19 mpg in the city and 21 mpg on the highway). Fuel delivery is through port direct-injection and twin-turbos. The impressive power numbers negate the need for aftermarket upgrades. However, many Bronco owners will still want to boost power output.

Cold-air intakes do contribute small horsepower gains. They generally make air-filter maintenance much easier and often have reusable filters. Several aftermarket companies offer cold-air intakes, including aFe, Roush, and Injen.

Air intake snorkels place the air intake near or above the top of the windshield. Originally intended for deep water crossing to keep water out of the engine and prevent hydro-locking, the cold-air intakes also keep fresh air intake above most of the dust on dusty, sandy roads and trails. Several companies offer snorkels with cold-air intakes, such as the Mishimoto snorkel and the Airaid snorkel kit.

Cat-back exhaust systems include the muffler behind the catalytic converter. Cat-back exhaust systems add small horsepower gains and can improve mileage. The exhaust tone is generally louder. Individuals may or may not enjoy the change in exhaust note. Flowmaster and aFe are two of several companies that offer cat-back exhaust systems.

and torque steer, and I was instantly off the track into the dirt—fortunately, not the wall. A major line alteration alleviated the issue.

To say the least: I'm not a fan of turbo lag, but after driving the 2.7L Wildtrak on the rocks, it turns out that the turbo lag can be a good thing. You really don't want (or need) tons of torque coming in instantly when crawling up a steep rock or ledge. The Ford engineers were either very clever or lucky, but either way, it works well for rock crawling.

Cold-air intakes and cat-back exhaust systems are available for the Bronco. The cold-air intakes and the cat-back exhaust systems add small power increases and are relatively easy to install. Snorkels place the air intake near the roof line, allowing cleaner air when driving in dusty conditions and keeping water out of the intake when fording water crossings. Corsa, Cobb, Mishimoto, Roush, Injen, aFe, K&N, and several other companies offer cold-air intakes. Borla, aFe, Magnaflow, Injen, Flowmaster, AWE, and others offer exhaust systems for the sixth-generation Broncos.

Engine tuning programmers can change the factory tune for the engine, usually increasing turbo boost and timing to add more power. Ford Performance, Superchips, RTR, Diablo Sport, Holley, Edge, and others offer performance tuners. More tuning products will become available as the aftermarket technology overcomes the restrictions on the computers and electronics on stock Broncos.

Engine cooling does not seem to be an issue with the sixth-generation Bronco lineup. Higher-flow radiator fans can improve low-speed cool-

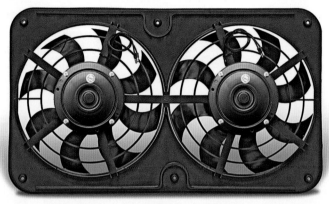

Engine-tuning programmers can increase power output and improve fuel economy. Changing engine parameters to achieve better performance can place more stress on the engine, which may accelerate wear. DiabloSport and Pulsar are two of several companies offering Bronco engine performance tuners.

If the use of the Bronco places extreme strain on the cooling system, such as driving at high altitudes, on steep grades, and towing heavy loads, higher-output cooling fans are available, such as this one from Flexlite.

V-8 engine swaps are very cool but also very expensive.

ing, especially when rock crawling increases engine loads and speeds are very slow, limiting airflow to the radiator.

As of mid-2024, a few brave souls have undertaken V-8 swaps for the Bronco using the Coyote engine. Most of the work is custom and requires significant fabrication. I have no doubt that some aftermarket companies will offer kits and complete installs in the future.

Transmission Upgrades

Several companies offer aluminum transmission pans, including B&M, PPE, and Mishimoto. Aluminum pans help trans oil cooling, but, more importantly, they increase protection for the transmission by replacing the original plastic transmission pan. Installing a transmission skid plate is still a good idea.

Adding a transmission cooler reduces heating of the transmission fluid when driving at very low speeds off-road. Mishimoto offers an add-on cooler.

For manual-transmission Bronco owners, B&M offers a must-have product. The B&M Precision Sport-Shifter for the 2.3L engine and 7-speed manual package provides a shorter throw and quicker shifts.

The Centerforce clutch and flywheel package provides much

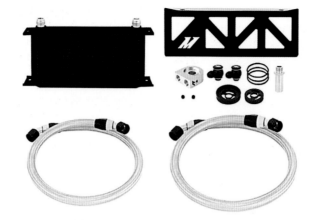

The low speeds when off-roading, especially on steep climbs and in rocky terrain, place high loads on automatic transmissions. Low speeds also mean that airflow is minimal. Additional transmission oil coolers can reduce transmission temperatures and increase transmission life. Mishimoto offers a selection of transmission coolers.

greater durability and the heavy flywheel makes low-speed rock crawling a breeze. Combined with the great crawl ratio of the manual-transmission Broncos, the heavy flywheel virtually eliminates stalling on extremely low speeds off-road.

Aftermarket transmission pans, such as this aluminum-finned model from Mishimoto, aid cooling but also offer puncture protection from rocks and sharp objects. While somewhat unusual, the stock Bronco plastic pan is vulnerable to punctures.

Turbocharger intercoolers add modest torque and horsepower gains by reducing intake inlet air temperatures. The Mishimoto intercooler kit for the Bronco 2.7L fits in the stock location, and the kit includes MWBK pipes and the intercooler.

The B&M Precision SportShifter for the modern Bronco platform with the 2.3L engine and 7-speed manual transmission includes a 303 stainless-steel stick with an anodized-aluminum pivot. The shorter throw between shifts allows quicker and smoother shifting. (Photo Courtesy B&M)

Off-road driving, especially rock crawling with a manual transmission, places significant strain on the clutch. Stock flywheels tend to be fairly light, making it difficult to control the throttle, clutch, and brakes at low speeds in the rocks. Engine stalling is very common in this situation. While the Bronco 7-speed manual transmission offers a very high crawl ratio in low-range first gear, a heavier flywheel and more durable clutch make low-speed crawling much easier. Centerforce clutches and flywheels provide a heavier flywheel and a much more durable clutch and pressure plate.

ELECTRICAL, LIGHTING, AND INTERIOR UPGRADES

Four-wheeling in the dark adds to the off-roading adventure. While the sixth-generation Bronco has excellent LED lighting, adding auxiliary lighting helps to brighten the road ahead. (Photo Courtesy Ford Motor Company)

Onboard computers control just about everything on the sixth-generation Broncos. Adding electrical components by tapping into existing wires can damage the computers. Auxiliary switching panels provide a multitude of safe options for engaging additional electrical components.

Ford offers a lighting package that helps owners avoid any electrical issues. The optional package on the Bronco offers excellent lighting capability. However, the factory optional lighting costs considerably more than some of the aftermarket auxiliary lighting solutions.

Auxiliary Switching Solutions

Off-roaders and overlanders will most likely need more auxiliary switches for lights, radio communications, compressors, and lockers. Broncos are equipped with auxiliary-switch options to cover most add-on electrical components. Several auxiliary-switch options are available from the aftermarket. Switch Pros offers high-end switch panels with mounting brackets and hardware specifically for the Bronco. Trigger Wireless Control Systems offers, as the name implies, a wireless four-switch panel for the Bronco.

Adding extra electrical components requires additional switches for control. Items such as light bars, fog lights, GPS units, radios, and other electronics place demands on the electrical system where extra switching power is needed. Switch-Pros offers an excellent kit with all wiring harnesses, mounting hardware, and even switch stickers, allowing customization. The control box is compact for easy mounting, and several mounting bracket options are available.

The Trigger wireless switching system eliminates the need to run wiring from the engine bay into the passenger compartment, simplifying installation. The Trigger systems add four switches for a variety of uses.

X Vision offers a large selection of lighting solutions. This light bar is mounted low, reducing aerodynamic drag and wind noise. Roof-mounted light bars often create serious reflection issues on the hood. This Bronco uses a flat black vinyl hood covering to reduce glare.

Auxiliary Lighting

As with many automotive electronic and electrical products, the lighting market has evolved with some very sophisticated lighting products, which are nearly all light-emitting diode (LED) based in today's market. For those not opting for the factory LED light option, many companies offer LED light packages that vary in price considerably. The Bronco LED package includes LED headlights and taillights, and LED fog lights and

Many companies offer cube lights. A bumper-mounted installation helps the light project below dust clouds when following other rigs on night runs.

daytime running lights are available on some models. Broncos can be equipped with a similar LED package, including only the headlights and fog lights. Premium LED lights are available from many aftermarket resources less expensively.

While the factory LED light option works great, additional auxiliary lights improve visibility at night, especially on difficult trails. The latest LED lights can be programmed to create a variety of lighting effects and even light shows. Some lights use smartphone applications for operation. Auxiliary lights come in several designs ranging from light bars of different sizes to driving lights, cube A-pillar-mount lights, fog lights, flush-mount lights, and rock lights. They are available in a variety of lighting patterns that range from narrow, long range, to wide. Some light bars use LEDs of various light patterns (wide as well as narrow). High- and low-beam functions are also found on some lights.

Light Bars

Light bars can put out tremendous amounts of light, especially the large (48-inch), roof-mount light bars. Smaller light bars can be mounted on the hood or bumper. Roof-mount light bars have several issues. The first is reflection off the hood. This can be distracting. Wind noise is another issue. Light bar covers can help reduce wind noise. Some states have laws limiting the height of light bars (or any auxiliary lighting) to at or below the level of the headlights. Some states allow the light bar to be covered when operating on the highway or streets.

Driving Lights

One advantage to driving lights is the compact size, which allows mounting to bumpers. A pair of bumper-mounted driving lights can be angled outward slightly to improve coverage. Driving lights are available in different lighting patterns and light temperatures.

Fog Lights

Several companies offer fog lights that fit in the stock fog-light receptacles. Many aftermarket bumpers feature openings and mounts for stock or aftermarket replacement fog lights.

Cube Cowl Lights

Cowl lights can also be angled outward, usually at a greater angle than driving lights to help illuminate the sides of a trail. This is especially helpful when navigating tight turns that are lined with obstacles. Several companies offer a wide range of cube lights and cowl mounts for the Bronco.

Cube cowl lights can be angled slightly to the outside to offer better visibility when turning, especially for the tight turns that are often encountered on off-road trails. Rigid Light is one of the premier lighting manufacturers in the US.

Light bars generate significant illumination to view the road and any obstacles. This light-bar system is from Project X.

Rock Lights

When rock lights were first introduced, they were viewed as being a fad. In reality, rock lights can be a great aid for rock crawling on night runs. The underside lights make it easy for a spotter to see obstacles underneath the vehicle. White-color lights are the most effective. As a side note, it is often best to minimize using really bright lights when a spotter is trying to see a rig. The bright lights can be blinding and cause misdirection.

The LED lights standard on Bronco models provide good lighting. Adding a light bar and other auxiliary lights really lights up the trail when the sun sets. (Photo Courtesy Ford Motor Company)

Daylight Driving on Dusty Trails

Dust can make visibility difficult during the day, especially to oncoming traffic. Run all lights during dusty conditions even in daylight. Another tip when off-roading in a group is to be careful how you use your auxiliary lights (unless you are the run leader). The drivers in front can be easily blinded by bright lights from behind.

Using lights in the daylight allows oncoming drivers to more easily see you. Following vehicles should also run with lights on in the daylight to allow the run leader to easily see the trailing vehicles on a run. (Photo Courtesy Ford Motor Company)

Dust makes visibility difficult even in the daytime. Light bars, cube lights, and driving lights may help visibility slightly, but the main reason to use them is to help warn oncoming drivers of approaching traffic.

Auxiliary lights are available from many sources. Many companies offer a wide range of light bars, driving lights, fog lights and cube lights. US-based companies, such as Baja Designs, Rigid, JW Speaker, and KC HiLites, all make premium lighting in a wide range of designs. Type S Automotive offers some innovative lights that can be operated and programmed with a smartphone application.

Radio Communication

CB (citizens band) radios were the go-to form of radio communication for many years. In recent years, ham radios have become very popular. Dual-band (UHF and VHF) radios with ham and commercial channels offer more frequency choices including non-ham channels, which do not require a ham license.

Due to short range, CB radios are becoming much less popular. General Mobile Radio Service (GMRS) radios are rapidly gaining popularity, especially with event organizers and clubs. GMRS radios operate on several different frequency ranges, including Family Radio Service (FRS) frequencies. GMRS radios require a license, but no test is involved like it is with a ham radio license. A license costs $35 for 10 years. No license is

Radio communication makes off-roading safer and allows easier discussion among members of a group run. While many old-school off-roaders prefer ham radios, the current popularity of GMRS radios makes them the best choice for most off-roaders. Midland offers a wide range of FMRS and FRS radios, including interior-mounted units (such as this) and handheld radios for easy portability.

needed to operate on the FRS frequencies. Midland Radios is on the leading edge of GMRS radios with a 40-watt version that has a range of 40 miles (line of sight). The Midland MXT400 is loaded with features, including 8 repeater channels and 15 high-power channels.

Satellite Messengers

Satellite messengers provide satellite communications via text message and emergency contacts with first responders. While it is always best to travel the backcountry in groups, the satellite messengers, including the Garmin InReach and the SpotX, make solo travel much more viable.

GPS and GPS
Smartphone Applications

Aftermarket GPS systems and apps designed for off-road travel generally provide more accurate and up-to-date information. The Magellan TRX7 GPS unit allows advanced trip planning and trip tracking. Several GPS apps use both iOS and Android operating systems for use on tablets and smartphones. GAIA, OnX Offroad, and Alltrails are designed for backcountry use. As reliable as modern GPS systems are, carrying a paper map as a backup is highly advised.

Batteries and Jumper Batteries

The addition of auxiliary lights, a winch, and other electronic devices puts a strain on the battery. Aftermarket batteries from Odyssey and Optima are designed to handle the additional electrical power requirements

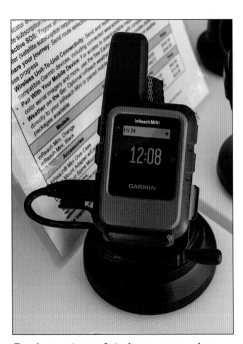

Backcountry safety has come a long way since the advent of satellite communicators, such as the InReach units from Garmin. They are equipped to send text messages and have an SOS feature to get help in an emergency.

Even if you have a factory GPS, the OnX Offroad smartphone application provides a vast array of trails and information. The smartphone application can be opened on the Bronco's infotainment system. OnX Offroad includes many features, including a route-planning component that is easy and intuitive to use.

GPS comes on many Bronco models and packages. For those lacking factory GPS, which is very good, Magellan offers a great GPS with the TRX7 system, which also functions as a tablet. Magellan provides an extensive library of off-road trails, simplifying trip planning.

Type S Automotive is one of several companies offering jump starters, which includes a power bank. The Type S Automotive unit is very compact, holds a charge for a reasonable duration, and (when fully charged) can jump start a vehicle three to four times.

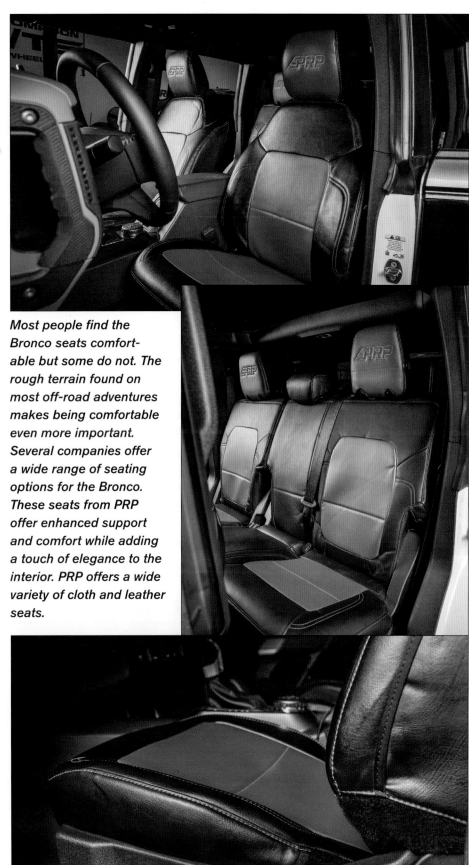

Most people find the Bronco seats comfortable but some do not. The rough terrain found on most off-road adventures makes being comfortable even more important. Several companies offer a wide range of seating options for the Bronco. These seats from PRP offer enhanced support and comfort while adding a touch of elegance to the interior. PRP offers a wide variety of cloth and leather seats.

and rigors of off-road driving. Many companies have entered the premium battery market with lithium batteries. They provide excellent power, are ideal for the electrical needs of overlanding, and are expensive.

Given the potential for battery overload or failure, carrying a jumper battery is a sound practice. Type S Automotive, among others, offers compact jump starters and power banks.

Interior Upgrades and Storage

Having secure storage in an off-road rig provides convenience and safety. Dozens of storage solutions are available to cover just about any need a Bronco owner may have.

Most off-road trails are bumpy. Staying comfortable presents a serious challenge. Good seating makes a significant difference. While Ford offers a good selection of seating options, the aftermarket offers a wide range of seating ranging from full race–style seats to very luxurious leather seats and trim.

ARMOR, PROTECTION, AND BUMPERS

Off-road driving presents many hazards. The potential for damage exists. While most Bronco models come from the factory equipped with some protection, additional protective equipment reduces the risk of damage to critical components and body panels. Different Bronco models come equipped with various protection, including skid plates, rock rails (rock sliders), and modular bumpers. Tube steps are offered as an option, but the tube steps offer very little off-road protection and are intended as a convenience option.

Skid Plates

Some Bronco models come equipped with skid-plate protection (called underbody protection or bash plates by Ford). The Bronco models with underbody protection include the Black Diamond, Everglades, and Wildtrak (optional).

The Badlands model includes six steel underbody shields, including the engine shield, transfer-case shield, fuel-tank shield, shin guards, stabilizer-bar shield, and heavy-duty front bash plate.

The Bronco skid plates use 4-mm (just over 1/8-inch) sheet-metal plates. While the stock skid plates offer some protection, even the Everglades edition with six skid plates could use improved protection. Other models with less protection need protection even more. Of course, if you never venture off-road, the protection is less necessary.

A few years ago, the stock underside skid plates offered adequate protection for easy to moderate trails. However, that's not the case today, as off-road trails and roads have deteriorated considerably. While it is a nationwide issue, the western regions have seen more profound negative effects. Several factors contribute to

Sixth-generation Broncos come equipped with some skid-plate protection, and steel bumpers are an option. While the stock components provide some protection, aftermarket bumpers, skid plates, and other protective parts offer superior protection. Upgrades protect the Bronco better if more difficult and extreme off-roading is on the agenda. Icon Vehicle Dynamics offers sturdy and stylish bumpers for the Bronco. (Photo Courtesy Icon Vehicle Dynamics)

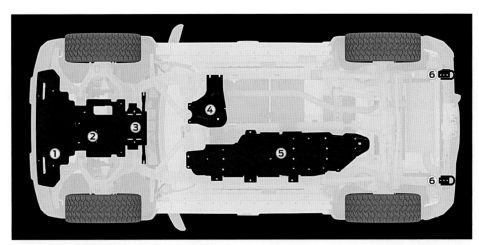

The stock skid plates on the Bronco include a splash pan that protects the steering and sway-bar disconnect (if equipped), the engine oil pan, transfer case, exhaust, gas tank, and tow hooks. The plastic transmission pan is not protected.

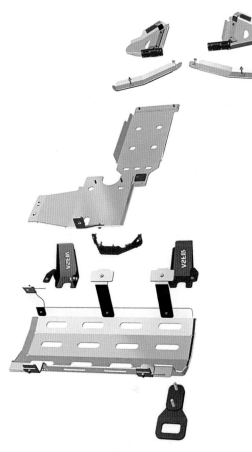

Left and above: ASFIR manufactures a full line of aluminum skid plates for the Bronco. The full skid-plate system provides complete underside protection. ASFIR also makes skid plates for the front lower control arms, lower shock mounts, muffler, and rear differential.

this decline: harsh weather causes more erosion and lack of maintenance by land-management agencies allows even more deterioration.

The influx of side-by-sides with different dynamics on the trails (lighter weight, a shorter wheelbase, and higher speeds) increase erosion by creating whoops and washboard sections. The increase of newcomers, especially in the side-by-side and overlanding segments, with little or no experience leads to poor driving practices, including having too much wheelspin, leading to increased trail deterioration.

Rock Hard 4x4 offers a full range of skid plates for the Bronco in steel and aluminum plate. The muffler on the Bronco is vulnerable to damage. Rock Hard 4x4 provides excellent protection for the muffler.

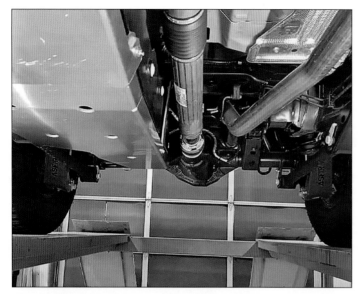

The ASFIR full belly-pan skid plate provides excellent protection for the gas tank. The aluminum plate construction keeps weight lower.

Full belly-pan skid plates from Rock Hard 4x4 offer excellent protection for the underside of the Bronco. Note the small trap door to accommodate easy oil changes and the tapered washers on the skid-plate bolts to resist getting hung up on rocks.

The trail deterioration causes more extreme ruts, bumps and exposed rocks. A little too much speed on an otherwise-easy route can lead to damage when an unexpected or unseen rut, rock, or bump can cause the vehicle to bottom out. Harsh impacts can lead to damage—not only to critical underside components but also to suspension, steering, and body sections. While the first line of defense is paying close attention, improved protection (not just underside skid plates) reduces the risk of serious damage when unexpected obstacles are encountered.

Rock Sliders

The rocker panels are easily damaged, and repairs are difficult and

Rock sliders protect the vulnerable rocker panels. The sliders protrude from the body to offer protection in the event of the vehicle tilting toward an obstacle. Rock Slide Engineering offers its slider step with an integrated swing-down step. Critics say this rock slider is not strong enough due to the internal step. I have used these slider steps on several vehicles in extreme rock-crawling situations where the sliders have taken a serious bashing, and I've never had an issue. Rock Slide Engineering offers an additional skid plate covering for the rock slider, providing even more durability and protection. Plus, the swing-down step offers ease of entry and egress for shorter occupants.

Rock Hard 4x4 makes a solid rock slider for the Bronco. The tubular slider protrudes away from the body, offering improved protection. The covering plate helps when entering and exiting the vehicle.

Ford offers optional rock sliders for all of the Bronco models.

expensive. Rock sliders, also called rock rails by Ford (or rocker slides), protect the vulnerable rocker panels below the doors. Rock rails come standard on Black Diamond, Everglades, and Badlands series and are a dealer-installed accessory on all other Bronco series.

Stock rock rails provide some protection. For more extreme off-road driving (even on deteriorating easy and moderate trails), more robust sliders are a great idea. Rock sliders take a real beating in more extreme situations. For this reason, they need to be made from durable, heavy-duty materials. Sliders can be made from formed steel, aluminum plate, or heavy-wall steel tubing. In addition, sliders should bolt to the frame rails. Some sliders have additional mounting points on the body to help stabilize the slider, but these can cause body damage and are less popular.

The stock rock sliders found on some Bronco models fit nearly flush with the body. While they offer protection from vertical impacts, they offer no protection to the side. For example, sliding off a rock sideways can cause the vehicle to tilt into a rock or tree. Rock sliders that protrude away from the body offer additional protection in these situations. Rock sliders are available from a wide range of aftermarket companies.

RockSlide Engineering's Slider Steps are a unique take on rock sliders, featuring built-in retractable steps. The RockSlide Engineering Slider Steps are very strong and even offer an add-on skid plate for additional protection in the rocks. At least a dozen companies offer rock sliders for the Bronco using formed steel, aluminum, and steel tubing.

Body Armor

Body armor protects the front and rear corners and quarter panels of the body. Armor is made from aluminum, steel, rubber, or plastic. Taillight and headlight guards are also available. While some of these products are heavy duty and can protect the body from dents, the primary job of this type of protection is to protect the paint and easily damaged components from scratching from rocks, heavy brush, and tree branches. Several companies offer a variety of body armor and protection.

Fenders

Aftermarket fenders offer additional tire clearance for larger tires and options to personalize the style

Opinions vary greatly on the stock Bronco fenders, especially on the Bronco Raptor. Lobo Off-Road offers attractive and sturdy carbon-fiber composite fenders for the Bronco.

Advanced Fiberglass Concepts offers a wide range of products for the full line of sixth-generation Broncos, including the Raptor. The product line includes fender flares, rear quarter panel kits (including fender flares), hardtops, and ram-air hoods.

for individual tastes. Both front and rear fenders are available in wide and narrow designs. The narrow designs do not cover the tires completely, causing water, mud and snow to spray. Many states require mud flaps if the tires are not fully covered by the fenders. Fender-delete kits allow the removal of fenders while hiding the mounting structure of the stock fenders. Fenders are available in many designs and in steel, aluminum, and plastic.

Bumpers

The Bronco offers a heavy-duty powder-coated modular steel front bumper with a heavy-duty bash plate standard on Everglades and available on all other Bronco models. Aftermarket bumpers are available in steel or aluminum. Winch-capable front bumpers facilitate winch mounting. Rear bumpers can be upgraded for more durability and to support the weight and size of larger tires.

Front

Front bumpers come in full width and narrow or stubby widths. Modular front bumpers allow a stubby bumper to become a full-width bumper (or something in between) by adding bolt-on sections to the narrow bumper. Most aftermarket front bumpers easily accommodate winches, lights, and D-ring or soft shackles for recovery.

Bumpers can be made from fabricated steel or aluminum, and they can be formed under extreme pressure from either material. Full-width front bumpers provide tire protection in brush but limit rock-crawling capability. Stubby front bumpers allow up to a 90-degree approach angle when climbing a single rock or when the Bronco is angled so that a large rock is approached one tire at a time.

Doetsch Off-Road designed a unique stubby bumper for the Bronco. The tube and plate design is lightweight and designed to accommodate a winch and lights.

Icon Vehicle Dynamics offers front and rear bumpers for the Bronco. The nearly full-width bumpers offer tire protection. The winch mount is low to keep the winch out of the airflow path to the radiator.

Icon Vehicle Dynamics's low-cost version of the Bronco bumper does not have the winch mount, but one can be added at a later date. The clean design looks good and is lightweight.

Most aftermarket front bumpers come equipped with shackle mounts. Bull bars, strikers, and stingers add additional protection for grilles and winches as well as good mounting points for lights. These add-ons are often options that can be bolted or welded to the bumper.

Rear

Rear bumpers are available in many styles. Rear bumpers need to be sturdy for rock crawling since they often impact large rocks when dropping off a rock or ledge, or can

The Rock Hard 4x4 Patriot full-width rear bumper is offered in aluminum and steel. The swing-out tire carrier is available on the steel version.

The Rock Hard 4x4 Patriot full-width front bumper offers an optional bolt-on winch mount and a bolt-on bull bar for mounting lights.

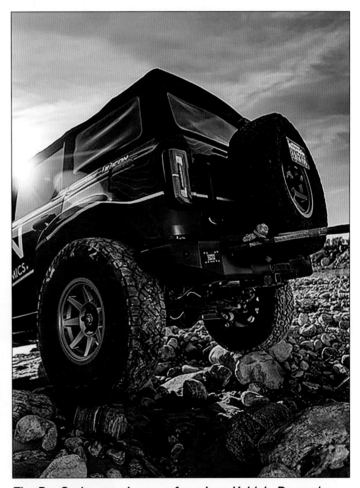

The Pro Series rear bumper from Icon Vehicle Dynamics features lightweight construction from a 3/16-inch steel plate, a favorable departure angle for good clearance off-road, and light mounts.

Rock Slide Engineering makes a nifty fold-down tailgate table. Made from aluminum, the table takes up very little space on the rear tailgate when folded but offers considerable room on the main fold-down shelf and extra room on the flip-up table cover.

scrape when climbing. Stock Bronco rear bumpers are easily damaged in these conditions. Most rear bumpers are designed to provide better departure angles than stock. Stock bumpers are not really suitable for extreme trail conditions. As with front bumpers, rear bumpers are made from steel and aluminum and can be fabricated or formed. Light mounts and D-ring and soft shackle mounts are included in some bumpers and optional on others.

Winch Mounts

Most aftermarket front bumpers feature mounts for winches. Some need additional plates to mount a winch. Be aware that not all winches have the same mounting bolt pattern, so check. Some winches will not fit on some bumpers due to clearance issues with the grille. Some front bumpers mount the winch low on the bumper keeping weight lower and improving airflow to the radiator. Winches place extremely

heavy loads on the bumper and frame. Be sure that the mounting points are very strong for the winch and bumper.

Tire Mounts

The sixth-generation Bronco spare tire mounts to the rear door. Some aftermarket rear bumpers include a tire carrier. Tire carriers come in two styles. Some swing out with the tailgate door, and others swing out separately. Those that swing with the door are more convenient but more expensive.

Other Mounts

Many rear bumpers have mounts (built-in and optional) for Hi-Lift Jacks, Pull Pal ground anchors, fuel/water cans/tanks, shovel and axes, and antenna mounts for GRMS or ham radios. These mounts can be very convenient for quick access and to keep some large, heavy items outside the passenger compartment, which enhances safety.

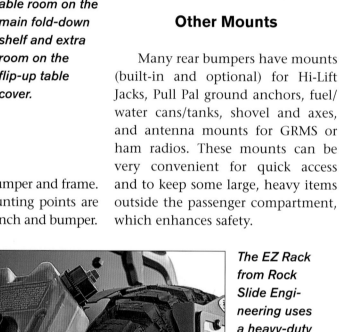

The EZ Rack from Rock Slide Engineering uses a heavy-duty ratchet tie-down around the spare tire to secure one or more mounting plates. The 10-gauge steel plates are formed to wrap over the tire tread and are slotted to hold a variety of items, including Roto-Pax liquid storage containers.

GETTING UNSTUCK:
VEHICLE RECOVERY TOOLS, WINCHING, AND RECOVERY TECHNIQUES

Getting stuck is part of off-roading adventures. It happens to everyone sooner or later. Vehicle recoveries offer challenges and can be fun especially when helping someone else get unstuck. Recovery gear provides many ways to get yourself and others unstuck with or without the assistance of another vehicle. However, keep in mind that vehicle recoveries can be dangerous. Exercise extreme caution.

Before delving into vehicle recovery and the important tools available to Bronco owners, let's take a quick look at common ways off-roaders can become stuck. Sooner or later, everyone gets stuck. Getting stuck is defined as the inability to move any meaningful distance either forward or backward. If you can back up from a situation, you are not stuck. You may not be able to move forward, but you are not technically stuck.

A single reason causes nearly all situations where a vehicle becomes stuck: lack of traction.

Vehicle recovery comes with the territory when off-roading. Being prepared with a solid recovery plan and a good selection of quality recovery gear makes recoveries more fun and easier, especially when recovering someone else's rig.

Traction loss resulting in the inability to move forward (or back) comes in two varieties: 1) loss of tire traction due to slippery surface conditions or 2) steep inclines or a loss of tire traction due to the vehicle becoming high-centered, creating drag and requiring even more traction to move forward. This takes weight off one or more tires, thus reducing traction even more. Most vehicles become stuck due to getting high-centered on bumps, exiting ruts, and on rocks. Sometimes a vehicle will get stuck when a tire gets too close to the edge of a rutted road section. The loose dirt at the edge can easily give way, causing a tire to slide into a rut.

Most recoveries are caused by these issues: a lack of traction or a mechanical breakdown. Traction loss can be caused by slippery surfaces (especially on steep climbs or rocks) and by getting high-centered, where traction is lost due to one or more tires lifting off the road surface. (Photo Courtesy Ford Motor Company)

The first agenda item in many vehicle recovery classes is the most important: how to avoid getting stuck. Here are a few principles to consider:

- When encountering slippery surfaces like sand, mud, snow (a little momentum helps), or ice (drive very slowly), look for the path offering the most traction, such as rocks or brush that may be protruding through the surface or along the edges of the trail.
- Avoid wheelspin. Some wheelspin is okay on soft surfaces if the vehicle keeps moving forward. If momentum is lost, wheelspin will only make the situation worse by digging deeper into the soil or snow. As soon as the vehicle comes to rest, lift off the throttle to avoid making the situation worse. The exception is when crawling on rock surfaces especially when wet, muddy, sandy, or snow-covered. Wheelspin could burn through the slippery surfaces, improving traction. This can also increase the temperature on the tire treads, which will also increase traction.
- Select lines in ruts and bumps that will keep the vehicle as level as possible.
- Approaching ruts and bumps at an angle (as opposed to a 90-degree head-on approach) will maximize ground clearance and reduce the risk of getting stuck. The best approach is to tackle a bump, ledge, or rut one tire at a time.
- If your vehicle feels "tippy," steer downhill. This could be on a side slope or when dropping down steep ledges or off of rocks. Steering uphill, which is a natural reaction, turns the downhill front tire into a fulcrum, making a rollover more likely. Turning downhill (or at least keeping the steering wheel straight ahead) allows the downhill front tire to act as a stabilizer.

- When steering, the rear tires do not follow the tracks of the front tires. In a tight, full-steering-lock turn on a four-door Bronco, the rear tires track a half width of the vehicle inside the front tires.
- When planning a line through rutted or rocky terrain where steering is involved, it is just as important (maybe more) to plan a line for the rear tires. Most drivers (and spotters) ignore the rear tires when planning a line through obstacles.
- Use a spotter (or at least get out of the vehicle to survey the situation) when the terrain becomes challenging and especially when driver visibility is limited to the sky and tree tops.

The second agenda item in the vehicle recovery classes relates to taking inventory of the situation, analyzing the situation, and then looking at recovery-gear options and what tool will be the most efficient and safest for the job.

Recovery Tools

Important recovery tools include a tow strap, shackles (soft and hard), a kinetic (yanker) strap, extraction (traction) boards, a shovel, off-road jack, winch, tree-saver strap, and winching anchor points.

Tow Strap

Tow straps are used for towing but can also be used for pulling a stuck vehicle out of a moderately stuck situation. Pulling out a stuck vehicle should be done with no slack in the strap (unlike a kinetic yanker strap). Tow straps have very little stretch. Use only tow straps with stitched material loops on the ends. Metal hooks tend to break under higher loads.

Tow straps come in several lengths. Twenty feet is the most common length. Use only tow straps with a stitched loop at each end (not a metal hook, as they are prone to breaking). Using a strap that is too long is a common mistake when narrow trails and tight turns are encountered. The towed vehicle may be pulled off the trail in tight quarters. Tow straps have very little stretch and should never be used for a kinetic or yanking recovery.

The most common straps are 20 to 30 feet long by 3 inches wide. For towing, the strap should be fairly short (no more than 20 feet), especially when towing in close quarters and with tight turns. Longer straps can get hung up in tight turns or pull the towed vehicle on an undesirable path, such as into a rock, tree, or soft shoulder.

A recent addition to the off-road tow-strap market is the kinetic tow strap. While the strap is kinetic, meaning that it has some stretch, the straps are only 10 feet long and are not intended for yanking (only towing). These straps offer two important advantages over standard, flat straps: 1) the short length allows maneuvering in tight quarters and 2) the slight amount of give softens the impact when slack is allowed to appear in the tow strap and suddenly the strap becomes taut. The kinetic tow straps are available from Yankum Ropes and Trail Mater.

Shackles

Shackles are used for attaching winch line or tow straps to a vehicle. Shackles must be rated stronger than the strap or winch line to which they are attached. Two types of shackles are commonly used. The most common is the D-ring shackle made of high-strength steel. Soft shackles are becoming more popular, and they are the best to use in most cases. Soft

Shackles are used to connect winch lines and to strap to a vehicle, tree-saver strap, or other stationary object. Shackles come in two styles: soft shackles and D-ring (or bow) shackles. Soft shackles are lighter, easy to use, and safer. I use D-ring shackles on vehicle-bumper shackle mounts, especially when the mounting hole has a square, sharp edge that will fray a soft shackle. A soft shackle is then used in the D-ring shackle.

shackles are made from the same synthetic materials that are used for synthetic winch line. If a D-ring shackle fails, it can cause damage or serious injury. Soft shackles are safer, easier to use, and lighter.

Many aftermarket bumpers have shackle attachment points. Many of the attachment holes have a sharp edge that can accelerate wear on soft shackles. I use D-ring shackles on bumpers and then attach the soft shackle to the hard shackle.

Kinetic (Yanker) Strap

A kinetic strap functions like a large bungee cord. When stretched, it stores energy. Unlike a chain, cable, or a nylon tow strap, which do not stretch much when a pulling force is applied, the kinetic strap is designed to store energy as it is stretched. Then, when it is snapped back, the effective pulling force is increased because the strap snaps back faster than it was stretched.

Kinetic (or yanker) straps are used to pull a vehicle out of a stuck situation by getting a running start. The kinetic strap, like a large bungee cord, will stretch under load. The stretching creates a kinetic load, which adds energy to help extract a stuck vehicle. If a vehicle is stuck in mud, sand, or deep snow and buried considerably (up to the axles or frame), a kinetic strap is dangerous to use, as the forces are very high. A winch is a much better option in this case.

Kinetic yanker straps are used to yank a stuck rig off of a dirt obstacle or out of mud, snow, or sand. Kinetic straps are not ideal for yanking a stuck vehicle out of a rocky situation. The forces are substantial, even though the kinetic shock absorption characteristics of the kinetic strap soften the blow. Attach the yanker strap with shackles to a secure point on each rig. Too much speed from the pulling vehicle can damage either vehicle and/or cause a shackle or strap to break, which can result in damage or injury.

Extraction (Traction) Boards

Extraction boards are best used when stuck in soft surfaces such as snow, mud, and sand. The lugs on the board are designed to engage with the tire tread. When the tires begin to rotate, the tire tread pulls on the lugs on the board. The boards then elevate the vehicle as it moves forward (or backward) and provide a solid surface to get unstuck. They are easy to use and are often the quickest way to get unstuck. They do not work on hard surfaces or rocks.

Most traction boards, such as the MaxTrax, are solid boards, using molded lugs to grip the tire tread. The newer MaxTrax designs feature metal lugs, which are much more durable. A new (to me) extraction board is the GoTread. The GoTreads are hinged, so they easily conform to rough surface and can be folded for easy storage. The GoTreads are also much less expensive, and they work!

Shovel

Shovels are most often used to dig out of the snow when stuck. Shovels are not much help in sand or mud. They are also used for digging holes to place ground anchors for winching. Folding shovels are very inexpensive and compact. More useful options include multi-tool kits, including the Hi-Lift Handle-All, which uses a telescoping handle and shovel, pick, sledge hammer, and ax head attachments. The MaxAx is a similar tool kit with interchangeable attachments. An inexpensive folding shovel is a low-cost alternative.

Many situations require a shovel or an ax. Multitool kits provide great versatility. The Hi-Lift Handle-All uses a telescoping handle and shovel, pick, sledgehammer, and ax head attachments. The MaxAx is a similar tool kit with interchangeable attachments. An inexpensive folding shovel is a low-cost alternative.

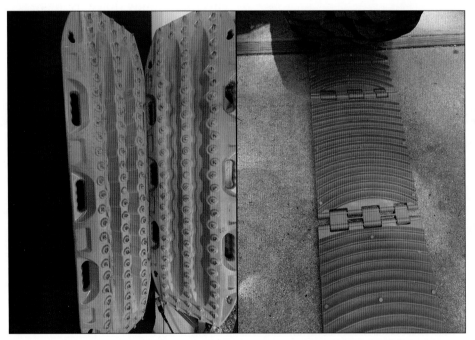

Extraction boards (or traction boards) can be placed partially under tires to gain traction in soft surfaces, such as snow, sand, and mud. The do not work very well on hard or rocky surfaces. The MaxTrax (left) was the first traction board on the market. They are very durable and work well in soft surfaces. The Go Treads (right) feature hinged panels, allowing the boards to conform to the road surface. In some cases, the Go Treads work extremely well.

Off-Road Jacks

Off-road jacks provide a means of changing a flat tire or gaining clearance under a tire when stuck. The Hi-Lift jack is the gold standard of off-road jacks. The Hi-Lift jack can be used in a variety of vehicle recovery situations as well as tire changing.

Hi-Lift offers many accessories as well. In recent years, many other off-road jacks have flooded the market. Many copy the Hi-Lift design, while others offer some innovative jacking solutions. ARB offers a hydraulic hand-cranked vertical jack that is easy to use, expensive, and a little bulky. Pro Eagle makes a traditional-looking floor jack with off-road-type wheels and tires. These jacks make lifting a Bronco really easy, but the cost is high and storage can be an issue.

While the vertical jacks work great for lifting, changing a tire is problematic due to the distance the body/frame must be raised to get the tire free from the road surface. Hi-Lift sells the Lift-Mate, which is designed to directly lift the vehicle from a wheel, greatly reducing the amount of travel up the jack bar needed to lift the wheel off the ground The Lift-Mate is also the quickest way to lift a vehicle that is high-centered on rocks, humps, or logs.

For changing a tire, a jack stand is needed to support the axle and tire off the ground so that the Hi-Lift jack can be removed to change the tire. The process is reversed to lift the vehicle off of the jack stand. Another option for tire changing is a compact, inexpensive bottle jack. A bottle jack can be placed under the axle housing near the offending tire to quickly lift the tire off the ground. I use a jack stand with a built-in bottle jack. The stand has a solid plate base to minimize sinking into the surface under load.

Winches

Winches provide an easy and efficient means to get unstuck whether you need a pull or you are assisting another off-roader. The sixth-generation Bronco provides winch-mounting capability for up to a 12,500-winch capacity. The standard plastic bumper on some models is not winch capable, but the modular bumper and the winch-capable bumper each provide for winch mounting. Most aftermarket bumpers are winch-capable.

Winches usually provide the easiest way to get unstuck in many situations. With the ever-increasing popularity of overlanding, many companies have entered the winch market. It can be difficult to know which winch will get the job done safely and over the long haul. Quality is important. The last issue anyone wants is a winch failure during a critical recovery process.

I have seen several winches fail during vehicle-recovery classes. The failure points are most often related to electrical wiring that shorts out. I always recommend quality winches, such as those from Warn, Nova Winch, Trekker from Rugged Ridge, Ramsey, Superwinch, and the Badlands from Harbor Freight (a low-cost alternative). Many economy brands are also available. For the more economical winches, I recommend using the winch at about half the maximum pull capacity. So, for a 10,000-pound economy winch, any pull estimated to exceed 5,000 pounds, I suggest using a snatch block to keep the load as light as possible to reduce strain on the winch.

Most modified Broncos weigh about 5,500 to 8,000 pounds. The minimum winch pull rating should

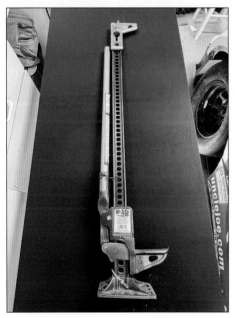

The Hi-Lift jack was created more than 100 years ago. The USA-made product has gone through many refinements over the years and has become the standard for off-road jacks.

The Warn competition winch on Loren Healey's King of the Hammers Bronco features Factor 55 end links and a hawse fairlead for the synthetic winch line.

Superwinch offers a line of winches with a variety of pulling capacity. A 10,000-pound winch works well for most Bronco applications.

The low-profile Westin winch bumper allows the Superwinch to be mounted low in the bumper, allowing improved airflow to the radiator. Westin manufactures the Superwinch and a complete line of bumpers and protection products for the sixth-generation Bronco.

Low-profile bumpers keep the winch low and tucked into the bumper for a clean look. The line attaching the end link to the winch line looks odd and may not be very strong.

Rough Country offers a line of less-expensive winches. If a winch is only used on rare occasions, the less-expensive models provide good service. The more-expensive, higher-quality winches, such as those made by Warn, Superwinch, and Mile Marker, are preferred for heavy-duty use.

be 9,500 pounds, and a 12,500-pound pull rating is more desirable. Keep in mind that the load on the winch is more than just the vehicle weight. The terrain is a significant factor. A pull on a flat, level, hard surface requires only about 100 to 200 pounds. The power needed to pull up a 45-degree slope with a smooth, hard surface is equal to the weight of the vehicle. If that surface happens to be deep sand, snow, or soft dirt, you can double the pulling power necessary. With a 10,000-pound-rated winch, you would need to add a snatch-block pulley to double the pulling power of the winch. The maximum pulling power of a winch occurs when the winch line is nearly fully unspooled with only one layer around the winch spool. When the winch line is fully wound, most winch lines will have four layers around the spool. The least pulling power occurs with the most layers of winch line on the spool. With four layers on the spool, pulling power is reduced nearly 50 percent or about 12 percent per layer.

Synthetic winch line offers equal or greater strength compared to steel winch cable. Synthetic line is lighter and does not store energy, so if it breaks, it is much safer but is considerably more expensive. The additional cost is worth the increased safety.

Winch Line: Wire Rope versus Synthetic Winch Line

Wire rope has a singular advantage: cost. Synthetic winch line is light and considerably safer. Synthetic line absorbs shock loads better, softening the abrupt loads as slack is taken up. The synthetic line is much easier to handle, especially when rewinding on the winch drum. Wire rope strands can break, causing potential gashes on unprotected hands. Synthetic line will not cause cuts when frayed. Synthetic line is thicker and has more tensile strength, so the length of line on the winch spool will be shorter than on wire cable.

Winch Controllers

Two types of winch controllers are commonly used. The most common is the plug-in remote, which attaches to the winch for operation. Wireless remote winch controllers use a signal from a handheld controller to operate the winch. The advantage to the remote winch controller is the ability to use it away from the vehicle out of harm's way. However, be sure to check that the controller battery is working before heading out on an off-road adventure.

Winching Accessories

Winch line end links connect the winch line to a strap or another vehicle. Most end links are hooks with a spring-loaded latch to retain the hook to its attachment point. Other end links accommodate closed winching system rigging. A closed winching system features connections with no openings, unlike those found on hooks. A hook with a sheet-metal, spring-loaded safety latch is not a closed-system connection. End links for closed system winching are available in several designs. Factor 55 is a leader in closed winching system recovery hardware. Closed winching system rigging is much more secure and safer.

Winch fairleads help control the direction and smooth flow of the winch line when spooled in. Two types of fairleads are used. The roller fairlead features four rollers around the perimeter of the fairlead mount and is used for wire rope winch line. A hawse fairlead is generally made from machined aluminum with a smooth, radius on the opening. Hawse fairleads are used with synthetic winch line.

Shackles are critical, as covered previously.

Snatch Blocks

Another critical accessory is the snatch block. A snatch block (or pulley) increases the pulling power of a winch. Snatch blocks can also alter

Snatch blocks (or pulleys) increase the pulling power of a winch and can be used to change directions of the winch line. Two styles of snatch blocks are used for different types of winch line. A retention ring or pulley is much lighter and easier to use compared to a traditional snatch block. Retention rings are only used with synthetic winch lines. Traditional snatch blocks work best with steel-cable winch lines.

the direction of the winch line (if necessary), when a straight-line pull is not possible. A new style of snatch block called a retention ring or pulley is much lighter and easier to use compared to a traditional snatch block. Retention rings look like a metal wheel with a groove for the synthetic winch line and a smooth center bore for a soft shackle. The soft shackle anchors to a tree-saver strap or a second vehicle while the winch line runs back to the winching vehicle for attachment to a shackle mount on a bumper.

Other Gear

Other important winching accessories include gloves to protect the hands and a winch line damper. Winch line dampers keep a winch line from flying, should the loaded line break. Dampers are important on any winch line, but critical on steel winch rope. Winch manufacturers offer both weighted dampers and dampers with pockets for weights like rocks or sand. An alternative to commercial winch line dampers is the use of a blanket, towel, or jacket on the winch line when the line is under load.

Tree-Saver Strap

Attachment points that are away from a vehicle (a tree, large rock, another rig, or other object) require strength and stability. Use care when selecting a winching point. The most common attachment point in the backcountry is a tree or rock. Never loop a winch line around a tree trunk or rock. You will damage the tree (often destroying it), and a winch line could pull under a rock, dislodging it and causing a serious problem.

In either case, use a strap (not a chain or cable) around the tree trunk or rock. In addition, if you really care about the environment, use a 3- or 4-inch-wide tree-saver strap. Wide tree-saver straps increase strength and spread the load over a larger area, which protects the tree bark and reduces chafing on large rocks. Many companies make wide tree-saver straps, including Gear America, Factor 55, Hi-Lift, and Warn. A bow shackle or soft shackle is then used through the loops at the ends of the tree-saver strap. The winch line end link or hook attaches onto the shackle.

Anchor Points for Winching

Winches are designed to pull in a straight line perpendicular to the centerline of the winch spool drum. Any variation from a straight pull places an increased load on the winch, the winch line, and other components, and it increases the risk of the recovery. If the winch line is being "bent" to either side by the fairlead (if it is rubbing or rolling on the side of the winch fairlead) the angle of the winch line is too great. This puts a lateral (sideways) load on the winching vehicle. Lateral loads will pull the rig sideways. Realign either the winching rig or the anchor point to get a straight pull. Ideally, the winch line should clear the side of the fairlead or hawse by at least one inch.

Angles too large can cause all sorts of nasty problems beyond accelerated wear and tear on the winch, fairleads, and winch lines. The side load creates a large additional drag component. Think of trying to pull a rig from the side and the furrows the tires would try to dig. Any angle from straight adds a sideways pull and increases resistance, and that sideways load puts a strain on the suspension, tires, wheels, and wheel bearings.

I have seen tires begin to unseat from the wheel beads with a nominal side load while winching up a steep incline. On a wide-open area, either sloped or flat, you may simply need to steer the rig that is being winched during the first few feet of pulling so that everything aligns properly. Be careful if you are on a steep slope: if the steering causes the winched rig to traverse the slope at even a small angle, a rollover becomes more possible. It is wiser to find an anchor point that better aligns with the winching process. The winch will try to align everything naturally anyway, but the real issues occur on narrow trails where there is no room to maneuver or steer.

Next, select an anchor point that will allow using most (but not all) of the winch line. Remember that a winch makes the most power with the fewest layers of winch line on the drum. As layers are added, the drum diameter is increasing, which changes the gear ratio of the winch and reduces effective pulling torque. The more load that you think the winch will be pulling, the more important it is to start with the fewest layers (one layer) of winch line on the winch drum as long as at least four wraps of winch line are around the winch drum. Never allow the winch to pull without several wraps on the drum. If need be, use a snatch or pulley block to allow more winch line to be unspooled from the winch drum. The key is to always survey the situation before you begin. Time is on your side. Haste in the beginning almost always costs more time than patience. Plus, it is much safer to take stock before you take action.

Multiuse Tool Kits

The Max Ax Tool kit is extremely versatile for a wide variety of trail needs—from digging out of sand, snow, and mud to chopping large fallen trees for easier removal from a trail. The ax head is permanently mounted to a stout fiberglass handle that has a spud for mounting the other accessories, including a shovel, rake, and a variety of pick heads. This is not a recovery tool that is needed often, but when it is needed, it's worth its weight in gold.

A Handle-All is a multi-functional tool with a telescoping handle and four full-sized implements, including a full-sized shovel head, sledgehammer head, ax head, and pickax head.

While flat tires do occur off-road, they are unusual with off-road tires rated at D, E, or F ply ratings, especially when the tires have been aired down. If a tire goes down the best options are to change the tire or plug the puncture with a tire puncture repair kit. Extreme Outback and Safety Seal make comprehensive tire repair kits. Simple kits are available from auto parts stores. A flat tire in a convenient location is contrary to Murphy's Law. It is extremely unusual.

A 35-inch-diameter mud-terrain or all-terrain tire mounted on the spare-tire carrier can weigh over 100 pounds. Even on flat, stable ground, that weight creates a difficult task. Imagine changing that tire on a loose-dirt hill with an off-camber slope. Just jacking the vehicle to remove the flat becomes dangerous. A tire repair kit can be used to plug a tire without jacking or removing the tire, and it can be done in any location as long as the puncture is exposed. Plugging the tire is easier and is usually quicker and much safer than trying to change the tire.

Occasionally, a flat is caused when the valve stem is damaged by

a rock or a shrub branch. There is a new product available to replace the valve stem from the outside of the rim. The Colby valve uses a unique design that secures the valve stem to the rim from the outside without removing the tire from the rim.

Recovery Techniques

This section covers how to estimate the winch's pulling load, how to use a tree-saver strap, when to anchor to another rig, and more.

Estimating the Winch Pull Load

Different situations, such as the slope grade and surface condition, affect the pulling load on a rig. Naturally, the weight of a fully loaded rig is the most obvious, and a good idea of your rigs laden weight is important.

For example, overlanding rigs weigh about 5,000 to 6,000 pounds, depending on the number of occupants and the amount of gear being carried. The surface condition is also a major factor. Smooth asphalt or concrete offer little resistance and, therefore, little pulling load. In fact, the resistance is only about 2 to 3 percent of the rig's weight (or about 100 to 180 pounds, using my rig as an example). That's not much load, but you get into soft surfaces, and rolling resistance goes up, as high as 50 percent of the rig's weight (2,500 pounds in my case). That does not take into account a rig stuck in the muck (snow or mud). The pull needed to free a Bronco that is stuck up to the axles or frame may be as high as 120 percent of the rig's weight.

The hardest pull that I have encountered was a 4x4 pickup that was stuck in soft, slushy snow up to the frame. A straight winch pull with

only a single layer of winch line on the drum would not budge the rig, even after an hour of digging snow away to reduce drag. After using a snatch block, the 9,000-pound winch was able to pull the rig free with an estimated load over 15,000 pounds.

For most soft surfaces, sand, snow, mud, gravel, and soft dirt, figure that the load will be about 25 to 30 percent of the rig's weight. That's about 1,250 to 2,000 pounds in my example. This is probably pretty close as an estimate for most backcountry trail situations—that is, until you're winching up a slope.

Intuitively, the steeper the slope angle, the more the load will increase. At 30 degrees, it is about 60 percent of the total weight of the rig, but at 45 degrees (a 1:1 grade), the load is 100 percent of the rig's weight. It goes up from there but at a slower rate. If you try to winch up a 60-plus-degree slope, well—don't! Take an alternate route.

Remember, you need to add the rolling resistance factor to the equation along with the slope. It's a tough pull up a 60 percent slope with soft surface conditions and a 5,000-pound rig using a 9,000-pound-rated winch.

Finally, most 4x4 electric winches are rated for an intermittent duty cycle, so if you have a long, hard pull, give your winch and battery a break once in a while. Let the motor and battery cool for a few minutes, and then resume the winching process.

Using a Tree-Saver Strap

As previously mentioned, a 3-inch (or larger) tree-saver strap is both stronger and less likely to damage sensitive tree bark. Straps can be used around trees, rocks, and even posts—although, not many posts are found in the backcountry. Make sure

Tree-saver straps protect the bark on a tree when the tree is used as an anchor point for winching. The wider the strap, the more the winching load is spread over the tree trunk, reducing the possibility of damaging the tree.

that the tree or rock is substantial. Small trees can become uprooted, and rocks can become dislodged. Unless you are trying to down a tree or move a rock, this is not a good thing. You really want to move the rig, not the anchor.

The tree-saver strap should be placed around the bottom of a tree trunk as close to the ground as possible, since this is strongest spot on a tree. The exception to this is if the tree is over the brow of a slope, where placing the strap higher will keep it off the ground. Watch the tree closely. If the load increases and the trunk begins to bend, you may need to move the strap lower on the trunk. Another exception occurs when the vehicle that is being winched sits higher than the ground where the anchor point is located. The winch will pull down on the suspension, greatly increasing drag. Placing the anchor point higher on a tree (assuming the tree is stout enough) can lift the front of the vehicle slightly and help pull the vehicle, especially if the winched vehicle is in mud or snow.

Use a towel or piece of carpet under the winch line where it rubs on the ground to protect the line, especially if it is synthetic rope. If you're pulling your own rig, the line is sta-

tionary as the vehicle moves (but if you pull another rig, the winchline moves since the winching vehicle is stationary). On a rock, attempt to place the strap below the waistline of the rock, so that if the strap does slip under load, it will slide down toward the ground (not up where it could slip off the rock).

After placing the strap around the object, make sure no twists are in the strap to reduce wear on the strap and minimize tree damage. Next, place the looped ends together and align the ends so that they are in line with the winch's direction of pull. Finally, insert the loops onto the bowed section of a bow shackle, and then insert the pin. Remember to tighten the pin until it bottoms. Then, back off about 1/4 to 1/2 of a turn to ensure that unscrewing the pin is easy when removing it (or use a soft shackle).

Anchoring to Another Rig

While other rigs do make good anchor points, they should not be your first choice. Since another rig may also be traction-limited, it could easily slide toward the rig being winched, even when in gear and with the brakes applied. This applies to a stationary rig attempting

to winch out another vehicle. I have had a rig chained to the back of the winching rig in both muddy and icy trail conditions, and instead of pulling the stuck rig, both stationary rigs moved across the slippery surface. Ultimately, I had to use a tree-saver strap around a tree down the road and then secure the winching rig to the strap with a length of heavy duty chain.

If a stationary rig is used, the driver should be in place, holding in the brakes with the rig in gear (if an automatic) and the engine running. Place wheel chocks to help keep the rig stationary. If the rig that is intended to remain stationary moves, cease winching immediately and try something different.

Using a Pull Pal Ground Anchor

The Pull Pal is a great tool. If you have nothing to pull against with a winch, the winch is useless. The Pull Pal provides an anchor point in cases where no trees, large rocks, or other rigs are available, and this happens more often than you might expect. If you drive in snow, sand, or desert areas, there are often no trees or rocks to anchor to. If you're on a narrow trail with a steep climb, even with other rigs, they may not be in a position to provide an anchor. Often, finding a suitable anchor that lines up adequately with your winch so that the pull angle is within an acceptable range can be impossible.

The one thing that is always available is ground, and it is rare to find solid rock trails with no rock outcropping to anchor to. I have used the Pull Pal in snow, ice, sand, dirt, loose dirt from mine tailings, gravel, and loose, small rocks. It has always dug in enough to easily pull

Ground anchors, such as the Pull Pal, allow a winch to be used when there is nothing available to attach the winch line to. The spade or shovel head attaches to an articulating arm, which allows the shovel head to be pulled into the ground with the winch. When the spade begins to dig into the surface, it allows the winched vehicle to move forward. The loads that a Pull Pal can create are impressive.

from, and it is easy to use—even though it is somewhat bulky by necessity.

The Pull Pal is a two-piece unit that folds compactly to the size of an ordinary bumper jack for easy storage. It can be mounted inside or outside, or it can be stored in an inexpensive case. The Pull Pal is ruggedly constructed with a forged chromemoly plow assembly and an articulating anchor frame with welded construction overall. The Pull Pal gets your rig unstuck by inserting the plow point into the soil. As the winch cable tightens, the point embeds itself deeply and firmly into the ground and frees your rig with the assistance of the winch and the wheels in motion. The Pull Pal can be used on the rear of the winching rig as an additional anchor when the surface is slippery. The more force that is applied to the Pull Pal, the deeper it imbeds itself into the surface, providing increasing anchoring security.

The two-piece assembly includes the plow head and the articulation anchor arms. The plow attaches to the arm via slots in the plow head and a slide-locking mechanism on the arm and head. No tools are required. The point of the plow head is then inserted into the ground with the arm assembly pointing toward the winch. The winch line hook is then inserted in the hole in the arm end. By tensioning the winch line, the geometry of the plow head and arm pulls it into the surface at an angle. More force on the winch secures the plow head more firmly in the ground.

The plow movement slows, and the winched rig begins to move forward. The head will be set, and you now have a very secure winching anchoring point. To release the Pull Pal, simply remove the winch line and lift up on the arm assembly until it breaks free of the surface. I have had situations where the plow head set so firmly, even in snow, that I could not pull it free by hand. I then placed the winch directly over the top of the arm end so that the winch pulled straight up on the arm. This easily released the plow head from the surface.

Using a Deadman Off-Road Winching Anchor

The Deadman Off-Road winching anchor works as an anchor point in a wide range of winching situations. The Deadman anchor is a large tarp (28 inches by 48 inches) and is made from industrial 18-ounce vinyl with rip-stop polyester, allowing it to conform to misshaped objects, such as rocks, without ripping. The 2-inch strap webbing uses Class VII industrial sling webbing, which is the same material used in industrial rigging and hoisting applications. Each line has a breaking strength of 19,600 pounds in a straight-pull configuration and 39,200 pounds in a basket configuration. Because the Deadman uses two of these, when both lines are in use, its breaking strength doubles, giving the Deadman a minimum breaking strength of nearly 80,000 pounds in a basket configuration.

Most often used in soft surfaces, the Deadman anchor works by being buried in the soft dirt, sand, or snow from 2 to 3 feet deep, depending on the softness of the material. Harder, more dense surfaces require a shallower hole than softer surfaces. Most assume the weight of the material covering the Deadman anchor basket provides resistance to winch against. However, the resistance is provided by the dirt, sand, or snow from the full depth the anchor is buried all the way to the winching point.

In other words, the Deadman anchor is attempting to compress many cubic yards of material. The Deadman anchor has be tested with pulls exceeding 7,000 pounds in soft surfaces. Due to the strength of the vinyl rip-stop tarp (basket), the Deadman anchor can be used around rock for an anchor. The Deadman also works great as a tree saver. The goal of a tree-saver strap is to protect the tree bark and spread the pulling load over a larger area to protect the tree. The Deadman anchor provides a very strong anchor point with a wide base which spreads the load over a greater surface area on the tree truck, protecting the tree and offering a high degree of safety. The strength of the Deadman Off-Road winching anchor even allows its use as a 15-foot winch line extension.

Winching Rules

- Never use a winch designed for off-road use as a hoist for lifting vertical loads.
- Never use a winch to lift a person.
- Always wear gloves, especially when working with wire rope. They fray and cause nasty cuts.
- Pull out the winch line from the spool by hand with the clutch lock released just in case the line was doubled over when rewinding. When doubled over the line suddenly reverses direction and gives the person pulling out the line quite a tug. The exception to this may be on a steep slope where the winch being used for recovery is on the rig stuck on the slope. The driver should stay in the rig if possible to hold the brake and ensure the rig remains stationary while someone else plays out the winch line. After the line is pulled out, the slope must be descended again to engage the clutch lock. In this case, it may be easier and safer to slowly ascend the slope as the winch operator runs the line out with the winch control.
- Keep everyone away from the swing zone of the winch rope.

This is the radius that the winch line could swing in if the connection were to break at either end. This zone actually has two radii (one at each end). The best place to be is to the side of either the rig being pulled or the anchor point, whether it's a tree, rock, or another rig. Anyone within the winch-line swing zone is at great risk if the winch line or any attached component fails. Synthetic winch rope is much safer than the more common steel winch rope, which, when under tension, can act like a very powerful sling shot—something you would expect to see on *MythBusters*. Be careful.

- After putting a little tension on the winch line, place a line damper on the winch line. This is really important when using steel winch rope, as it is not self-damping like synthetic winch rope. A winch line damper is any fabric weighing at least 4 to 5 pounds that can be draped over the winch line. Should the line snap, the damper will minimize the snapping effect of the broken line and reduce the flinging of the line itself or items attached to it. A damper could be a large towel, jacket, blanket, sleeping bag or a special winch line damper designed for this purpose. While synthetic winch line is much less dangerous, it can't hurt to use a damper on it as well.
- Assign tasks to all who are available. Make sure someone is positioned to watch the vehicle being winched to make sure that there are no binds or other potential problems. Someone else can watch the anchor point, especially if this is another rig. Make

sure everyone is on the same page for communication verbally and with hand signals. Keep it simple, like a thumbs up and verbal "okay" for pulling and a "stop" with a balled fist thrust into the air to stop winching. The driver of the rig with the winch doing the pulling should be responsible for organizing this. Make sure the observers are out of harm's way before beginning the winching operation.

- Always have at least four wraps of winch line around the drum before winching. This is the minimum to ensure no slippage of the line on the drum.
- A winch design follows the laws of physics. As layers of winch line accumulate on the winch drum, pulling power decreases. Winch power can be reduced nearly 50 percent from maximum when the line is five layers thick versus the single layer with a starting point of five wraps on the drum. If you have a difficult pull, play out the winch line as much as possible to maximize the pulling power. If necessary, use a snatch block in order to play out more line. The pulley will also double the pulling power while reducing line speed to half.
- Most 4x4 electric winches are rated for an intermittent duty cycle, so if you have a long, hard pull, give your winch and battery a break once in a while. Let the motor and battery cool for a few minutes, and then resume the winching process.
- If the winch line is dragging on the ground over a slope breakover, use a piece of carpet or towel to minimize the wear on the line as it drags on the dirt or rocks.

- After checking all connections, lightly tension the winch line and then recheck every connection and make sure everyone is in a safe location and ready to start pulling.

Road Building

If you get stuck on a trail due to a high-centered situation or when trying to crawl over a steep rock and traction is lost, road building is likely the best solution for getting beyond the difficult spot. Most often, road building is altering the contour of the trail to gain ground clearance under your rig or to build a ramp up a steep boulder to reduce the angle of attack. This is done by using trailside rocks, tree limbs, or bridging ladders.

There are three distinct scenarios. First, if you continue driving, you will hit the underside of your rig without altering your line or increasing ground clearance. If you continue onward, you will likely become high-centered, which is the second scenario. Third, you encounter a large rock you must crawl over to continue forward, but the lack of traction and the steepness of the boulder halts your forward progress.

In the first case, you can either alter your path, or back up and build up the trail so that you have more clearance when the obstruction is approached. Doing this before getting high-centered is easier and reduces the chance of rig damage. Position the rocks or limbs so that the tires can drive over them in a way that allows increased ground clearance.

If you do get high-centered, you can try reversing off the obstacle, but this could cause damage, so analyze the situation carefully first. If available traction is too little for this, the first inclination is to pull

the stuck rig, either with a tow strap or a winch, to free it from the obstacle, and this will often work, but the damage risk is much higher. It is almost always best to use a Hi-Lift jack to raise one or more tires and then build up the trail under the tires to gain the needed ground clearance. Make sure that your new section of road is stable.

If you come up to a boulder you must crawl across but it is too steep or you lack adequate traction to ascend it, try building a ramp with rocks to reduce the angle of attack up the rock face. Otherwise, use bridging ladders if you are carrying them. You will not usually need to use a jack for this process.

Here are some tips:

- Always wear gloves when road building.
- Have someone assist you in moving large rocks—they're heavy!
- Be aware of your fingers when moving rocks—they can be crushed.
- A spotter should communicate to the driver when crossing the new section of road that you just built.
- Keep clear of the new road buildup when the driver takes off. Rocks can move or be thrown, causing injury.

Be creative in your problem solving, but also think through what could happen before you take action. It almost always pays to take the most conservative action that will get you going again, even if it takes a few minutes longer.

Winter Recovery

Recovering a stuck rig in the winter is much more difficult and more likely. Snow is the perfect medium for

getting stuck and comes in so many forms that it's impossible to describe them all. In fact, the Eskimos have 100 words describing various types and qualities of snow.

A rule of thumb for snow depth is to avoid roads where snow depth or the tracks in the snow from previous travelers is so deep that your frame, bumpers or any part of the vehicle drags on the snow. Short-distance sections, a few feet are okay if only a few inches deeper, but long distances through chassis deep snow will cause build up under your rig and you will get high centered on the accumulation. That can be a real pain to get out of, even if you have a winch. Snow surfaces change, especially on warmer days. The hard crust in the morning or late evening can soften. What would support you earlier may allow you to sink in and possibly become trapped, so it's good to know the area you're driving, the grades of the trail, which can be much more problematic than flatter trails, the snow conditions, and weather forecast.

Then there's ice! Iced-over trails can be nearly impossible to navigate especially on climbs and treacherous on descents. Take extreme caution and drive slowly when it gets icy, and look for a path along the trail where traction may be better, such as the edges of the trail where rock or brush may be protruding.

Finally, you will likely encounter slippery, gooey mud. Like snow, it comes in many varieties.

Always carry plenty of provisions (water, clothes, blankets, and other survival gear) just in case.

Travel with another rig. The more difficult the trail and the conditions, the more important this is. Be well-equipped. Four wheeling in the winter is great fun, beautiful and challenging, but it can turn disastrous quickly, so be prepared. Remember that a lack of preparation can open the door for Murphy to implement his annoying law.

So what equipment do you need to carry? I have used every piece of gear that I have on winter recoveries, sometimes on a single recovery. Here is what's mandatory.

At a minimum, carry a set of chains. Preferably, carry two sets of chains so that you can chain up all four tires. You'd be amazed at how well you can climb icy slopes with all four tires chained up. I've even towed disabled rigs up icy slopes with chains.

Take along the standard stuff you should always have anyway, such as a Hi-Lift jack and accessories, a tow strap, shackles, and a shovel. Don't forget the shovel! Digging out of snow with your hands is no fun!

In the winter, a winch is invaluable; it is by far the easiest and quickest way to get unstuck. Make sure you have a tree-saver strap and a snatch block. Pulling a rig out of deep snow can create huge loads, so be ready and be very careful. Winch line loads can easily exceed 10,000 pounds when pulling out of deep snow.

A ground anchor, such as the Pull Pal, is invaluable. Even in the mountains with lots of trees and rocks, I got stuck on a road in snow with nothing to pull against. I got a Pull Pal the day before, and I loaded it almost as an afterthought. Including figuring out how to use the Pull Pal, which was pretty simple, I was out in less than 20 minutes. The Pull Pal dug in so solidly that I had to position the winch over the end of the Pull Pal to pry it free, which turned out to be easy and effective.

An ax and pick can be very handy for breaking up ice, which can happen even in fresh snow when the hot driveline melts snow and then it refreezes into much nastier ice or a hard pack.

I also found bridging ladders to be really helpful for ramping up out of snow or crossing narrow gullies from spring melt runoff. I don't use them often, but when I need them, they are invaluable. This, as with a Pull Pal and other big-ticket items, can be shared by a group. Not every rig on a backcountry expedition needs every item, but always carry the basics yourself so that you are prepared for most situations, including being stranded overnight. Watch out for Murphy—be prepared! Then, you can enjoy the beauty and challenge of winter backcountry adventures. In addition, remember the shovel!

Towing a Disabled Vehicle

Most breakdowns can be flat-towed to a spot where a tow truck can tow the vehicle for repairs. There are several exceptions:
- Steering system failures (a tie-rod or steering rack)
- Some situations with broken suspension arms
- Broken hubs or steering knuckles where the wheel/tire cannot rotate normally
- Broken axles
- Crash damage which prevents the tires from rolling

In these situations, trail repairs or an off-road tow truck or trailer may be needed.

Tow Straps

Tow straps should have a rating of at least 20,000 pounds of breaking strength with stitched end loops

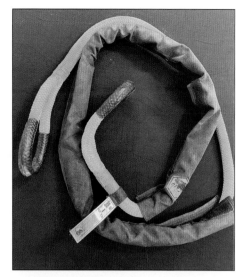

The Trail Mater kinetic tow strap (made by Yankum ropes) is actually a 10-foot-long tow strap made for towing in tight quarters. The kinetic stretch of the strap is minimal but does soften the shock load when the towed driver cannot maintain tension on the rope and the slack is suddenly taken up.

Standard tow straps for off-road use, such as these from Hi-Lift are available in a variety of lengths. Shorter straps are preferred in tight quarters, which makes it less likely that the towed rig will be pulled off the side of the trail. Longer straps are best in desert environments, where turns are generally more gentle. Longer straps are also beneficial on hill climbs and rocks, where the towing vehicle may be able to get to flatter ground before the towed vehicle encounters the obstacle.

(not metal hooks). A minimum of a 2-inch width is required. Do not use a kinetic (yanker or snatch) strap for towing unless the kinetic strap is very short (10 feet) and intended for towing. The stretch of a longer kinetic strap can make the towing operation more difficult with damage more likely. Purchasing a strap made by a company specializing in off-road recovery gear is best.

Tow-Strap Length

The standard lengths for straps are 20 feet and 30 feet. Longer straps allow a greater safety margin between the towing vehicle and the towed vehicle. Shorter straps allow much better maneuverability in the tight quarters that are often found on off-road trails. The longer strap can pull the towed vehicle into obstacles or the edge of the road when making tight turns. A 20-foot strap allows better maneuvering in tight quarters. A 30-foot strap that is doubled-up to 15 feet in length is even better. When towing straight ahead, the longer strap may allow the towing vehicle to clear a rock allowing a better pull for the towed vehicle over the rock obstacle.

While I do not recommend kinetic straps for towing, there is one exception. Trail Mater (through Yankum Ropes) offers a 10-foot kinetic tow strap in 5/8- and 3/4-inch diameters that is designed for towing. The small amount of stretch softens jerky motions a little but not enough to upset the towed vehicle. This strap works great in tight quarters.

Tow Strap Rigging

The tow strap should be attached to the towing vehicle to a receiver hitch shackle and to a tow point on the towed vehicle bumper. Using soft shackles is best. While using tow hooks will work, using a closed-system tow point is best.

Communication

Good communication between the towing and towed drivers is a must. Radios are best. Horn honks are good for attracting attention. Hand signals are good when used by the driver of the towing vehicle to the trailing driver, but not so great when used by the trailing driver. Both drivers need to be on the same page to avoid confusion or problems.

The Job of the Towing Driver

The towing driver sets the pace, which is very slow. When making turns, the towing driver needs to swing wide so that the towed driver can make the turn more easily without getting dragged into an obstacle, the edge of the road, or running over the tow strap. To indicate that the towing rig is slowing, the driver should apply the brakes with his or her left foot so that the brake lights appear before slowing the vehicle. This provides advance warning to the driver that is being towed.

The Job of the Towed Driver

The most important job is paying complete attention. Second-most important is keeping the tow strap tight with no slack. While the towing driver controls the speed, the towed driver should be the one slowing both vehicles with the brakes (unless on a very steep descent).

Dealing with a Broken Tie-Rod

A broken tie-rod means that only one front tire steers when the steering wheel is turned, which is not conducive to meaningful movement. Getting a rig with a broken tie-rod off the trail takes massive effort—unless, of course, you carry a spare tie-rod, have an onboard welder, or can use a section of tubing to sleeve over the broken section of the tie-rod. A few sections of angle iron can be used to cover the broken section. Heavy-duty hose clamps can hold the angle-iron sections in place. It's not an ideal setup, but it's workable at very slow speeds.

For the sixth-generation Bronco, the best course of action requires replacing the stock tie-rods with much stronger aftermarket tie-rods or a bracing kit to strengthen the stock tie-rods. The fragile stock tie-rods are prone to failure, so carry a spare stock tie-rod at the very least. If you upgraded to aftermarket tie-rods, keep the stock tie-rods and bring them as backups.

OVERLANDING

What elements define overlanding? Overlanding requires the use of a mechanized vehicle (as opposed to human- or animal-powered travel). It includes mountain bikes, motorcycles, and four (or more)-wheeled vehicles. Overlanding also requires complete self-sufficiency. This is similar to backpacking, where the participant must carry food, water, shelter, clothing, and hygiene supplies for the duration of an adventure.

Unlike backpacking, overlanding requires participants to also carry fuel, tools, for repairs as well as tools for getting unstuck, navigation gear, and communication devices. For the most part, overlanding uses unpaved roads for travel and avoids developed campgrounds or RV parks for camping.

Off-highway travel is paramount to overlanding, and the off-highway travel makes overlanding a subset of off-roading in general. By definition, off-roading is the use of a motorized vehicle off paved routes and usually on public lands. Public land may be managed by the United States Department of Agriculture (USDA) Forest Service, the Bureau of Land Management, or state, county, or municipal agencies. Off-roading often also occurs on private land, usually in off-road parks, especially east of the Mississippi.

So how does the sixth-generation Bronco fit into the world of overlanding? Nearly all Bronco models make outstanding overlanding rigs. The Bronco offers plenty of storage, has power to carry the loads needed for overlanding, and can easily tow an overlanding trailer. Add the Sasquatch package to the mix, and the Bronco can access many thousands of miles of off-road trails for exceptional adventures.

Many longtime overlanders do not consider themselves to be part of the off-roading community. This belief can lead to ignoring some of the basic ethics and courtesies long established for using motorized vehicles on public lands. Non-adherence to the rules, laws, and courtesies that have long guided the off-road community can lead to route closures and disasters.

Overlanding, or vehicle-assisted adventure travel (back in the day, it was called "car camping") offers the Bronco owner the opportunity to explore incredible backcountry locations. The sixth-generation Bronco is an ideal rig for overlanding.

Storage needs make vehicle section an important consideration. Sixth-generation four-door Broncos have excellent storage for extended overlanding adventures. It is important to keep heavy gear as low as possible in the vehicle to maintain a low center of gravity to aid stability, especially off-road. (Photo Courtesy Tyler Sasaki/Power Tank)

Clever storage solutions make overlanding gear storage secure and easily accessible. Slide-out trays allow quick access to often-used items. Many aftermarket companies offer great storage solutions. Many overlanding enthusiasts with good woodworking or fabrication skills create their own storage. (Photo Courtesy Tyler Sasaki/Power Tank)

Propane is the fuel of choice for overland cooking, and fire extinguishers are must-have items for off-roading. Power Tank makes a compact interior mount to hold propane and a fire extinguisher (specifically for the Bronco). (Photo Courtesy Tyler Sasaki/Power Tank)

Airing up is a critical element of overlanding. The Power Tank allows rapid and easy airing up. The mounting bracket from Power Tank holds 10-pound Power Tanks and a Pro Eagle bottle jack. Secure storage is critical for the rough terrain that is encountered when overlanding. (Photo Courtesy Tyler Sasaki/Power Tank)

Some definitions of overlanding suggest that an overlanding trip must be a long-term adventure lasting more than a few days. However, weekend or even one-night adventures in the backcountry certainly qualify as overlanding. Some overlanding die-hards would have you believe that fully decked-out rigs are a necessity. That is also untrue. Any vehicle with good ground clearance driving on easy routes in dry weather can be used for overlanding. While four-wheel drive is desirable, it is not needed on easy terrain when the roads are dry. Two-wheel-drive trucks, vans, and SUVs will work. All-wheel drive is helpful, and four-wheel drive is desirable. Good, high ground clearance is mandatory because low-ground-clearance

This display shows a wide range of storage options, including Molle panels, shelves, racks, fold out tables and Molle-capable storage bags.

The RotoPax fuel cans are mounted on a RockSlide Engineering EZ Rack, which provides mounts conforming to the spare tire. The rack is held in place by a sturdy ratchet strap. Several companies offer a wide variety of racks that mount to the spare tire.

vehicles are susceptible to underside damage and easily become stuck on rough terrain. Here are some items needed to participate in overlanding adventures:

- A vehicle with good, high ground clearance (such as the sixth-generation Bronco)
- Food storage
- Water supply
- Some type of sleeping gear
- Food preparation gear or pre-packaged food items
- Additional clothing and layers for cold weather

Rooftop tents are a great sleeping option for overlanding. Clamshell tents provide good accommodation, are easy to set up and store, and can be very low profile, offering less wind resistance. The downsides of a rooftop tent includes raising the center of gravity (decreasing lateral stability), and they are expensive. (Photo Courtesy Tyler Sasaki/ Power Tank)

A rooftop tent (or a ground tent) is pretty much a requirement for overlanding with a two-door Bronco. Soft-sided rooftop tents are more spacious but add more weight. Setup is slightly more involved. Access via a ladder requires some degree of nimbleness. This tent from Yakima is mounted to a roof rack also from Yakima. This type of integrated system ensures a solid, secure mount to handle highway speeds. (Photo Courtesy Ford Motor Company)

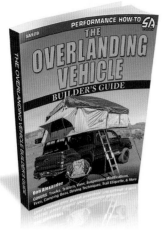

Overlanding has become incredibly popular. This chapter barely scratches the surface of this topic. For more great information on overlanding, scan this QR code to check out my book The Overlanding Vehicle Builder's Guide *from CarTech.*

- Physical maps or GPS-based smartphone map applications for a phone or tablet

Of course, this is a minimalist list of items, but it is all that is really necessary for warm weather and easy, dry roads and trails. A Bronco and minimal gear allow one to set off on an overlanding trip. This approach is a great way to start out to determine if overlanding is an activity to pursue. However, overlanding can be expensive. Modifying a Bronco vehicle can cost thousands of dollars even before investing many more thousands into cool overlanding gear.

If you are new to overlanding, here are several questions to ask yourself:

- How capable is your current vehicle? If your current rig is a sixth-generation Bronco, you're all set.
- How much off-roading experience do you have?

- What type of terrain would you like to tackle (easy, difficult, extreme, mountains, desert, etc.)?
- How comfortable do you wish to be while exploring?
- What is the longest adventure you would like to tackle (weekends, weeklong, monthlong, or yearlong)
- What is your budget?

If you have never been on an overlanding adventure, taking a short overnight or weekend trip will help you decide if overlanding is something you want to pursue, and it will hopefully answer some of the key questions. Look online for overlanding or off-roading spots close to home. Chances are good that you will have a great time even on a short adventure.

If you are an experienced off-roader with a well-equipped Bronco but have no overlanding experience, pack some food and a sleeping bag and tent and give it a try. You probably know of some great dispersed camping spots along some of your favorite trails. Otherwise, tackle those trails that are too long to complete in a day trip.

Overlanding, expedition travel, or backcountry adventure camping has been popular for decades. Today, the popularity of overlanding is increasing almost exponentially. Overlanding offers a great way to explore and is family friendly. I will touch on overlanding gear here, but the topic is so broad that it doesn't do the subject justice. My book *The Overlanding Vehicle Builder's Guide*, which is available from CarTech, provides more details.

Tents

For decades, tent camping was the shelter of choice for vehicle-based travel and camping. Modern popup

tents that require just a few seconds to deploy and stow are common. Dozens of companies make these tents. Other popular tents attach to vehicles, either using the bed of a truck or the back of an SUV as a sleeping area. One of the concerns about ground tents is wild animal attacks. Attacks on humans are extremely rare; attacks are even more rare on humans in tents. Mosquito bites are much more deadly. A rollover accident is much more likely with heavy gear or rooftop tents on the top of a Bronco.

Rooftop tents have grown in popularity by tenfold in the last decade. Many designs are available from a multitude of manufacturers. The one common denominator among rooftop tents is the necessity of climbing a ladder for ingress and egress. The only real drawback is the increased center-of-gravity height, which can cause instability in rugged terrain and additional wind resistance. Limits to the weight on Bronco roofs should be followed to minimize possible damage and to avoid failure while moving.

Ford rates the roof of a Bronco with a factory rack at a maximum load of 110 pounds dynamic and 450 pounds static when evenly distributed. In addition, if an extended stay in a camping spot is part of the plan, using the vehicle to explore local areas or set out for supplies requires packing up camp, including stowing the rooftop tent.

Off-Road Trailers

Off-road trailers offer many advantages for overlanding adventures. Any Bronco model can easily tow an off-road trailer. More storage area, improved stability, and the ability to disconnect the trailer while

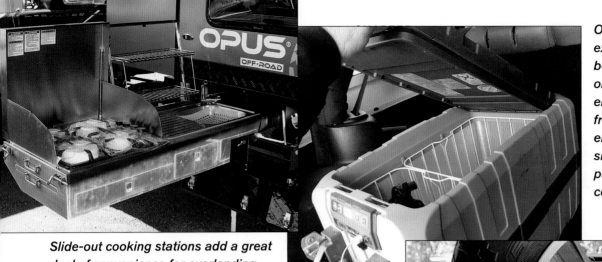

Slide-out cooking stations add a great deal of convenience for overlanding. This unit comes as standard equipment in the OPUS off-road trailer.

Overlanding trips exceeding a day or two benefit greatly from an onboard electric refrigerator, such as this one from Type S Auto. Refrigerators come in several sizes and many price points from a variety of companies.

Finding shelf or counter space for food preparation and other miscellaneous chores can be challenging. The Rockslide Engineering Tailgate mounts to the tailgate and unfolds to make a two-tier shelf/counter.

Bolt Lock offers a selection of strong locks. They utilize a unique feature which allows the lock to be programmed for use with the vehicle's key. Cable locks, spare-tire locks, and trailer-hitch locks are some of the locks available from Bolt Lock.

exploring a local area all enhance the experience; cost is not an advantage.

Off-road trailers come in three basic configurations: small trailers with a rooftop tent on a rack, soft-side pop-up styles, and hard-side trailers. Hard-side trailers offer more privacy and improved comfort and protection. Some campgrounds do not allow soft-side tents or trailers. Many companies in the US and Australia manufacture a wide variety of off-road trailers in different configurations, sizes, and floor plans.

Coolers and Refrigerators

Perishable food and cold beverages are mainstays of overlanding and day trips as well. Cold storage is just about a requirement for any off-road adventure. The most common cold storage source is the traditional hard-shell cooler packed with ice or freezer ice packs. Soft-shell coolers, such as the AO Coolers original soft cooler with high-density insulation, are becoming more popular. I have used the Arctic Ice cooler ice packs in place of ice for several years. They will last at least a few days, depending on the ambient temperature.

Refrigerator/freezer units are pretty much required for extended

overlanding trips. Several companies manufacture 12-volt plug-in refrigerators, most with 110-volt power supplies. Some also offer freezer capabilities. I have been using the Type S Blizzard Box for about two years with great results. Refrigerators come in several sizes and capacities. Prices range from around $400 to $1,500. Type S, Dometic, and Rough Country are popular brands for overlanding.

Security

Theft is rarely an issue in the backcountry, but the story is different in civilization. Many overlanding (and other) items are exposed on the outside of a rig, including the spare tire (in many cases). Locks provide an additional layer of security. I have

used the Bolt locks ever since they arrived on the market several years ago. Not only are they quality locks but the lock key is also your vehicle key. No need to lug around additional keys to unlock and gain access to expensive gear.

Bolt offers a variety of locks for the sixth-generation Bronco. Bolt offers padlocks, cable locks, 1/2- and 5/8-inch hitch receiver locks, trailer-hitch coupler pin locks, and a coupler lock for fifth-wheel trailer kingpins.

TOPS *By Matt Ross*

One of the biggest selling features for the sixth-generation Bronco is the option for an open-air experience. Depending on the trim level, some four-door versions have an option for a factory-equipped soft top that folds open or a hardtop with removable panels. The two-door version is only available from the factory with a hardtop. Each is also completely removable. Both styles allow a wide-open view to the sky—just in different ways. There are pros and cons to both. The aftermarket also has several options of hard and soft tops, including soft tops for the two-door version.

Factory Soft Top

The factory soft top has latches at the windshield that allow the area over the driver and passenger compartment to be quickly folded open without tools. The rear cargo area windows are vinyl and are removable, as is the rear window. Once the windows are removed, the entire top can be folded back, resting above the tailgate opening if desired. Another feature of the factory soft top is its ability to hinge up slightly at the

The factory soft top has a squared-off roofline at the rear, whereas most after-market full-soft-top options have a slope at the rear that follows the lines of the sport bar. (Photo Courtesy Ford Motor Company)

rear, allowing items slightly taller than the cargo area opening to be placed inside.

One complaint that many owners have of the factory soft top is that the vinyl side windows appear to sag, mostly due to the soft top's ability to hinge at the rear. In addition, the vinyl windows need to be very carefully removed to avoid breaking the clips that hold them,

and the windows are susceptible to scratches. Care must be taken when cleaning or storing the vinyl windows. As with all soft-top vehicles, factory soft tops are less secure and are made with a vinyl-like material that allows more interior noise, but they are quicker to open and close than removing and reinstalling the hard-top panels. It comes down to personal preference.

Factory Hardtop

Hardtop availability from the OEM supplier to Ford was an issue upon the launch of the sixth-generation Bronco. Originally, two options were available: the molded in color (or MIC) and a modular hardtop. The modular hardtop was almost immediately postponed due to production issues and was not made available until the 2024 model year (and only as an option on certain special editions). These are painted and have removable windows.

The MIC top became the only hardtop available for the first three model years but also had issues. Rough edges and inconsistencies in the outer shell layer led to cracking and a condition known as "snake skinning," where the outline of the honeycomb inner structure was visible. Colors often didn't match on the removable panels as well. This led to long delays on vehicle orders with a hardtop initially. Dealers strongly suggested customers switch their orders to a soft top just to get the vehicle built. Most of those issues have been sorted, but these are items to watch for on early-model-year sixth-generation Broncos.

The four-door versions have three easily removed panels, and the cargo shell can be unbolted and removed. The front two panels can be removed to open the area only above the driver and passenger, or all three panels can be removed to completely open the front and rear seat area. The two-door Broncos only have the two removable panels over the front seats, and the cargo shell can also be unbolted. The passenger panel removal is easy and toolless.

One downside to removing the hardtop panels is that they are a little

This is a four-door Bronco Raptor with the black appearance package. With the hardtop on and windows up, these are very quiet vehicles. Hardtops are available with a sound-deadening material as well to further quiet and insulate the interior. (Photo Courtesy Ford Motor Company)

The hardtop panels can be removed and stored in the cargo area, although this takes up a lot of room, especially in a two-door Bronco. Storage bags are available, but unless you are concerned with the weather, it may be best to leave them at home or at camp to avoid damaging them. (Photo Courtesy Ford Motor Company)

bulky to store in the vehicle, but Ford offers bags specific to the panels to store them in. Many leave the panels at home (which helps keep them from damage when they are removed), but not having the top panels means that you have no protection from rain. That makes the marine-grade vinyl seats and wash-out floor options worth having.

Aftermarket Tops

Aftermarket soft-top options are available from companies such as Rampage, Rugged Ridge, and Bestop.

The only option for a soft top on a two-door Bronco is from the aftermarket, as Ford does not offer an OEM option, although it does sell the Bestop Trektop and many other aftermarket products through its accessory department. These are also available from your favorite 4x4 shop or online retailer. Many prefer the look that these offer, as they have a slant at the rear that follows the angle of the roll bar. This offers a different look than the factory soft top, which helps to personalize the Bronco. These easily fold open over the front seats, and the Bestop opens over the rear as well on both the two- and four-door versions. The rear windows are removable (just like the OEM top) to fully open the interior.

Other top options that are very popular with hardtop owners are the Bestop "Sunrider for Hardtop" and Skyrider. These utilize the existing hardtop cargo-area shell but replace the removable panels with a folding soft top. This allows you to quickly and easily open and close the area above the passenger area without having to remove, store, and protect factory removable panels.

Other options are bikini/bimini tops. These are available from many aftermarket companies and are available in solid vinyl to completely shade the passengers when the top is open or removed, or they are available in a mesh material. The mesh is popular, as it provides some shade but still allows for airflow. Some can even be found with custom printing of various logos.

As of this writing, several aftermarket companies are getting close to releasing a hardtop. These will likely have a slightly different look from the factory hardtop options with similar options and functionality. As this generation of Bronco was completely new, the aftermarket companies need time to engineer something as involved as a full hardtop. Keep and eye on the internet, as options will become available.

Another top option is complete removal of the top. All sixth-generation Bronco tops (factory and aftermarket) can be fully removed, completely opening the interior to the elements. This changes the look of the Bronco. Pair this with the fact that the doors are designed to be easily removed. This provides the most open-air experience that is available.

Aftermarket tops, such as this Bestop Trektop, can be folded open and the rear windows removed for a complete open experience. These can also be used in conjunction with a mesh bikini to add some sun protection while enjoying the open air. (Photo Courtesy Bestop)

The rear of the Bestop Trektop follows the angle of the rear sport bar, which is a very popular look. They fit tight, and with upgraded material options, such as twill, are quieter and more durable than the factory soft tops. (Photo Courtesy Bestop)

The Bestop Trektop easily folds back, fully opening the passenger compartment. The rear windows can be left in (as pictured) or removed to completely open up the interior while leaving the top folded up and out of the way. (Photo Courtesy Bestop)

The Sunrider for the two-door Bronco takes the place of the two removable panels. Not only does it open and close quickly but it can also offer added trail visibility. (Photo Courtesy Bestop)

The Bestop mesh safari bikini top offers shade while still allowing full airflow. Think of it as sunscreen for you and your interior. (Photo Courtesy Bestop)

The Bronco Raptor is shown with its top and doors completely removed. The lower profile of the sport bar gives the sixth-generation Bronco an aggressive, almost "chopped roof" look. (Photo Courtesy Ford Motor Company)

The four-door Outer Banks version of the Bronco is shown with top completely removed. (Photo Courtesy Ford Motor Company)

The Bestop Skyrider replaces all three removal panels on a four-door Bronco, allowing quick and easy open-air access while keeping the hardtop rear shell. This allows for added security in the rear and the convenience of the factory glass rear hatch. (Photo Courtesy Bestop)

Bestop's Sunrider for Hardtop is similar to the Skyrider but only replaces the front two panels, opening just the area above the front seats. These are popular, as they are more cost effective, and they open the area where it matters the most (above the driver and passenger). (Photo Courtesy Bestop)

BRONCO OFF-ROADING TIPS

The sixth-generation Broncos feature several electronic controls to make use of two-wheel drive, four-wheel-drive high range, and four-wheel-drive low range as well as the G.O.A.T. modes and Trail Drive features. All of the features enhance the off-road capabilities of the Bronco. Learning to use them properly increases your enjoyment of the Bronco off-road experience. View chapter 2 for more information on using these controls. If you recently purchased your Bronco, there is a good chance the salesperson did not go over the 4x4 controls. Read the owner's manual. The same applies to used vehicles.

Visual Fields

Where you look is often where you go. Most off-road newcomers have a tendency to look right in front of the hood. Expand your visual fields to take in the terrain as far in front of you as possible. In addition, look at the terrain to the sides and to the rear. A trick is to rotate your side mirrors downward so that you can see the rear tire contact patches in rocky terrain. Keep your eyes moving and attempt to anticipate the terrain and the line you need to drive to avoid obstacles and stay safe.

Many trails are narrow and traverse shelves. Inattention even for a split second creates a situation where a tire can breach the edge of the road. This can lead to getting stuck or going over the side. Lack of attention can also allow a bad line into ruts, bumps, whoop-de-doos, rocks, tree stumps, and other unfriendly objects, leading to damage and a very unpleasant ride.

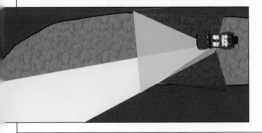

Steering Wheel Hand Placement

The driver's hands should be positioned on the steering wheel rim. Thumbs should be on top of the rim, not wrapped around the rim as shown here. Steering wheel kick-back over rough terrain can cause injuries to thumbs and wrists.

Place Tires for Ground Clearance

Straddling obstacles is intuitive for most new off-road drivers. Going for ground clearance reduces the chances of getting hung up or high centered on obstacles or even damaging critical underside components. Place tires on the obstacles to gain ground clearance. By practicing tire placement on small rocks, you learn where your tire contact patches are located. Knowing how much ground clearance you have is also helpful. If in doubt, reduce speed and place tires on the rock or obstacle. This is especially important to protect the stock tie-rods on the Bronco.

Look for Traction

Different surfaces have varying degrees of traction. Surfaces that provide good traction in the dry provide less in the wet and mud and even less in snow, and traction can be non-existent on ice. Sandy sections have less traction than dry dirt, which has less traction than rocky terrain. Brush and debris along the edges of a trail may protrude through ice, snow, or mud and can improve traction. Look for traction when the vehicle slips and slides and excessive wheelspin begins.

Disconnect Sway Bars

Sway bars control body roll when cornering on the highway. Limiting body roll on the highway is important, but when you are off-road, sway bars limit axle articulation. If the axles cannot move freely up and down, lifting one or two tires off the ground in big ruts, bumps, and rocks is likely. You can see this happening in some truck and SUV television commercials.

For safety (and lower blood pressure), keeping all four tires planted on the ground is a sound idea. Disconnecting the front sway bar reduces the likelihood of lifting tires off the ground and teeter-tottering. In rare cases, a rollover is possible. Disconnecting the front sway bar is most important. If you have a Bronco Badlands model, you have an electric sway-bar disconnect. If not, sway-bar disconnect kits are inexpensive solutions. Check out the full-length articulation and sway-bar-disconnect videos on Trails 411.

Spotter

The 360-degree cameras on the Bronco help judge the terrain as obstacles are approached. However, when the terrain is complicated, the line is difficult and the driver cannot see as well as needed, using a spotter is a sound idea. A spotter becomes the driver's eyes outside the vehicle. A spotter can see obstacles and determine the best path when the driver is unable to see the terrain. Spotters should use clear, concise hand signals when the vehicle is moving and only use verbal communications when the vehicle is stationary.

Learn Basic Navigation

All Ford Bronco models feature the Ford CoPilot 360 Technology, which includes navigation. In addition, Apple CarPlay and Android Auto are compatible, and other navigation smartphone applications, such as OnX Offroad, can also be used. GPS provides valuable information for off-road navigation. However, electronics can fail. Always carry a paper map for the area where you travel off-road and learn how to read a map and the basics of navigation. Free paper maps are available from most government land managers, such as the US Forest Service Motor Vehicle Use Maps (fs.fed.

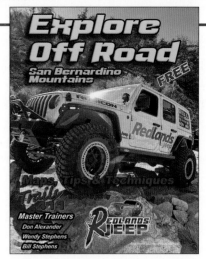

us/recreation/programs/ohv/ohv_maps.shtml) and the Bureau of Land Management (blm.gov/maps). Paper maps are available at visitors centers, ranger stations, and field offices.

Travel in Groups or File a Flight Plan

It is always prudent to travel in groups in the event of problems, such as getting stuck, breaking down, or medical emergencies. Club 4x4 runs and professional events, such as Bronco Jamborees or Trail Hero, are a great way to learn the ropes. If you want to go solo, satellite locators can help keep you safe in the case of an emergency. At the very least, notify someone you can count on about your planned route and estimated time of return. If you fail to report by a designated time, they can look for you or contact authorities.

Bring a Tow Strap and Shackles

Getting stuck comes with the territory off-road. It is naive to count on traffic to help out if you get stuck or suffer a breakdown, so be prepared. A good Samaritan passing by may be willing to help, but don't expect them to have a tow strap and shackles that are needed to get pulled out of trouble.

Carry the following items with you: a tow strap (use only tow straps with stitched loops at the ends, never straps with metal hooks because they can fail and are dangerous) and quality bow shackles or soft shackles. For more information about vehicle recovery, see chapter 11.

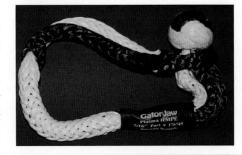

Carry a First-Aid Kit

The most dangerous element of off-roading is scampering around on rocks, hills, and ruts. Scrapes and cuts are fairly common. A basic first-aid kit is a necessity for backcountry travel. Fortunately, Ford offers a good first aid kit as an option on the Bronco. Learning first aid is a really good idea. At the very least, read the instructions in your first aid kit before using it for real. First-aid smartphone applications, including the SAS Survival Guide, can provide guidance.

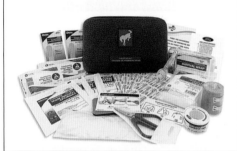

Angle through Ruts

Getting high-centered on bumps and ruts is both annoying and embarrassing. You can minimize the risk by crossing bumps and ruts at an angle. The goal is to place one tire at a time over the bump or through the rut to maximize ground clearance. In a series of undulating ruts and bumps, try to take the line that will keep the vehicle as level as possible.

Stay on Designated Routes

If a route is not marked or on an official map, it is probably not a legal route. Stay on legal routes. One of the biggest threats to motorized vehicle access on public lands is travel on illegal routes. If you're not sure, don't go.

Speed for Hill Climbs

Most hill climbs are best undertaken at low speeds (3 to 6 mph). Very steep hills (those steeper than most newcomers are comfortable tackling) need a little more momentum. Wheelspin should be kept to a minimum with a light foot on the throttle. Know what is at the top of the climb, even if it means hiking to the top. Many climbs require a sharp turn as the climb is crested. Missing the turn or carrying too much speed can lead to a very uncomfortable and dangerous ride.

Pack out Trash

Leaving trash in the backcountry leads to off-road areas being closed. Carry out any trash that you create, and help out the environment by picking up trash that has been left by thoughtless individuals. You would be shocked by the gross items that people leave behind.

Gear/Transfer-Case Ratio

Newcomers always ask what gear to select in the transfer case. Never use four-wheel drive on dry pavement. I always recommend four-wheel drive on the dirt for improved control. High range is fine for most situations but use low range when climbing or descending hills, especially steep hills. Use four-low range in rocks where speeds are low. If the engine speed exceeds about 3,000 rpm in top gear in low range, it is time to stop and shift back into high-range four-wheel drive. Use a transmission gear that keeps your engine speed near optimal torque (usually between 1,500 and 2,500 rpm).

Downhill Braking

Driving down steep hills causes weight to transfer off the rear tires onto the front tires. Braking causes more weight to transfer forward. The reduced weight on the rear tires makes them prone to lockup. If the rear tires lock while steering, the rear of the vehicle can begin to slide sideways. If uncorrected, the tires can catch in the dirt, rocks, or ruts, causing a rollover. This can happen even with antilock brakes. Counter-steering the wheel and easing off the brakes allows the sideways slide to be corrected. Very gentle acceleration can also help. Carrying extra speed may be uncomfortable, but that is preferred over tipping over. The Trail 1-Pedal Drive feature on the Bronco can be used to make navigating steep descents much easier and safer.

Dropping Down Ledges

Hard braking is required when dropping down ledges or off of rocks. The tires should roll down very slowly, not bounce on the springs. Weight transfer off the rear tires occurs when descending. Even more weight transfers forward if the front tires bounce down hard. Rollovers have occurred on steep drop offs where too much speed was carried.

An additional factor occurs when one tire drops down before the other. The natural tendency is to steer toward the uphill (or higher) tire. If the right front tire drops down before the left, the driver's first instinct is to steer left, but this causes the right front downhill tire to become a fulcrum. This will make a rollover more likely. Keeping the steering wheel straight reduces the risk. If possible, steering downhill (in this case) to the right helps to stabilize the vehicle and reduce the risk of a rollover even more. While the Bronco Trail 1-Pedal Drive feature helps in these situa-

tions, using the brake pedal may be a better option if the drop-off is steep and more than a few inches down.

Steering

While how much and when to turn the steering wheel seems basic, some elements of steering are not intuitive. Off-roading often requires full lock steering maneuvers in tight quarters. If the steering wheel is turned too much too soon, body damage can occur against trees, rocks, brush, and other obstacles.

When steering, the rear tires do not follow in the tracks of the front tires. The rear tires will track inside the path of the front tires. The sharper the turn the more pronounced this becomes. The rule of thumb for short-wheelbase rigs like two-door Broncos is to begin rotating the vehi-cle when the obstacle is at the A-pillar of the windshield. For long-wheelbase vehicles, such as the four-door Bronco, rotation should wait until the obstacle is at the B-pillar (or the driver's shoulders).

The Bronco offers a unique Trail Turn Assist feature that reduces the turning radius of the vehicle by applying the brakes to the inside rear wheel in low-speed, high-steering-angle maneuvers. Use it to get through switchbacks and around obstacles without executing multipoint turns.

Front Tires

Rear Tires

Left-Foot Braking

Left-foot braking enhances driver control when climbing rocks, dropping off ledges, and even climbing rutted hills. Power is controlled by applying pressure on the throttle pedal while controlling speed by modulating pressure on the brake pedal. An additional benefit of left-foot braking preloads the driveline (axles and driveshafts), reducing the risk of twisting a driveshaft or breaking an axle.

Sixth-generation Bronco models with the 2.7L and 3.0L EcoBoost engine with the optional automatic transmission offer Trail Drive technology, including the Trail 1-Pedal Drive feature. The 1-Pedal Drive (when activated) applies the brakes automatically when the throttle pedal is released and releases the brakes when the throttle is reapplied. This feature works in a manner similar to left-foot braking, but does not allow as much control as left-foot braking when used by a driver who has mastered left-foot braking techniques.

Fire Safety

Check fire restrictions in your area before traveling. Many areas have fire restrictions, which, among other things, do not allow campfires. Below is a USDA Forest Service Order for the San Bernardino National Forest as an example:

Current Fire Restrictions and Related Prohibitions

"The following acts are prohibited on the San Bernardino National Forest:

This Order is effective December 21, 2022, through December 31, 2023.

1. Building, maintaining, attending, or using a fire, campfire, or stove fire except in Forest Service–provided campfire ring or in a standing grill within a Developed Recreation Site. 36 C.F.R. § 261.52(a). A Developed Recreation Site means an area which has been improved or developed for recreation. 36 C.F.R.§ 261.2.
2. Smoking, except within an enclosed vehicle or building, a developed recreation site, or while stopped in an area at least three feet in diameter that is barren or cleared of all flammable material. 36 C.F.R. § 261.52(d).
3. Operating an internal-combustion engine anywhere other than on paved, gravel, or dirt National Forest System roads and trails, except boats on a water surface. 36C.F.R. § 261.52(h).
4. Welding or operating an acetylene or other torch with an open flame. 36 C.F.R.§ 261.52(i).V."

Most National Forests provide access to roads open to SUV and four-wheel-drive vehicle travel. The designated road system offers a wide range of experience levels, including novice, intermediate, and expert levels with signs for easiest, more difficult, difficult, and most difficult.

Green Circle (Easiest)

These fun family trails are suited for a stock vehicle and may not always require four-wheel drive. They are very well maintained. These roads are typically wide enough to accommodate passing.

Blue Square (More Difficult)

While more challenging than the easy-rated trails, drivers of all skill levels can enjoy these trails. At this level a stock high-clearance four-wheel-drive vehicle is required.

Trails are typically narrow with possible brush that may scratch your vehicle. Passing usually requires backing up.

Difficult

Trails at this rating require a vehicle with increased ground clearance and proper protection. Trails will often require a spotter and should only be attempted by more experienced off-road drivers. On most trails at this level 33-inch tires and at least one locker are recommended.

Black Diamond (Most Difficult)

Trails at this rating require a heavily modified vehicle.

Some damage to your rig is likely. Front and rear lockers, 35-inch tires, and a winch are highly recommended.

Most difficult-rated trails should only be attempted by the most experienced four-wheelers.

Trails become more difficult in adverse weather, such as snow and rain. Be prepared.

Other trail rating systems go into more detail (the Trail Rating System below) but are basically very similar. Always determine the trail difficulty before setting out on that trail. Most backcountry vehicle recoveries are for vehicles that are not suited for the rating of the trail. Be prepared, both for the vehicle, including recovery gear, and, as a driver, for the trails you plan to drive.

Trail Rating System	
Many backcountry trails use a more precise 10-level trail rating system.	
Rating	**Details**
1	• Graded dirt road • Dry (or less than 3-inch) water-crossing depth • Gentle grades • Two-wheel drive works in all conditions except snow • No width problems (two vehicles wide)
2	• Dirt road • Dry (or less than 3-inch) water-crossing depth • Some ruts • Slight grades (up to 10 degrees) • Two-wheel drive works well in most conditions • Rain or snow may make four-wheel drive necessary • Usually one-and-a-half to two vehicles wide
3	• Dirt road • Rutted, washes, or gulches • Water crossings (up to 6-inch depth) • Passable mud • Grades (up to 10 degrees) • Small rocks or holes • Four-wheel drive is recommended, but two-wheel drive is possible under good conditions and with adequate ground clearance and skill • No width problems for any normal vehicle • Vehicle passing spots frequently available if less than two vehicles wide

4	• Rutted and/or rocky road • No shelves but rocks up to 9 inches • Water crossings (usually less than hub deep) • Passable mud • Grades moderate (up to 15 degrees) • Side hills moderate (up to 15 degrees) • Four-wheel drive under most conditions • No width problems, vehicle passing spots frequently available if less than two vehicles wide 
5	• Rutted and/or rocky road • No shelves • Rocks up to 12 inches and water crossings (up to 12 inches with possible currents) • Passable mud • Moderate grades (up to 15 degrees) • 6-inch holes • Side hills (to 20 degrees) • Four-wheel drive required • No width problems 
6	• Rocky or deep ruts • Rocks (up to 12 inches) and frequent • Water crossings (may exceed hub depth with strong currents) • Shelves (up to 6 inches) • Mud may require checking before proceeding • Moderate grades (up to 20 degrees) • Side hills (may approach 30 degrees) • Four-wheel drive necessary and second attempts may be required with stock vehicles (caution may be required with wider vehicles) 

7	• Rocks frequent and large (12 inches) and may exceed hub height • Holes frequent or deep (12 inches) • Shelves (up to 9 inches) • Deep mud (8 inches) and may be present on uphill sections • Grades (up to 25 degrees) and side slopes (up to 30 degrees) • Water crossings (up to 18 inches and may have strong currents) • 1½ vehicles wide • Four-wheel drive required • Driver experience helpful 
8	• Heavy rock and/or severe ruts • Rocks exceeding hub height frequent • Shelves (up to 12 inches) • Deep mud or uphill mud sections • Steep grades (up to 25 degrees and can be loose or rocky) • Water crossings (may exceed 30 inches in depth) • Side hills (up to 30 degrees) • One vehicle wide • Body damage possible • Experience needed • Vehicle modifications helpful.
9	• Severe rock (over 15 inches) • Frequent deep holes (over 15 inches) • Shelves (over 15 inches) • Mud bog conditions (long, deep, no form bottom) • Water crossings (over 30 inches with strong currents) • Steep grades (over 30 degrees) • Side slopes (over 30 degrees) • May not be passable by stock vehicles (experience essential) • Body damage, mechanical breakdown, and rollover probable • Extreme caution required
10	• Severe conditions • Extreme caution recommended • Impassable by stock vehicles • Winching required • Trail building necessary • May be impassable • Impassable under anything but ideal conditions • Vehicle damage probable and personal injury possible • Extreme caution necessary

Trail Difficulty *continued*

Trail Rating Considerations

While trail ratings can be very helpful, they can vary from place to place. What may be a 5 rating at Johnson Valley could be a 4 rating at Sand Hollow or Moab. Try watching a trail video of a trail you plan to tackle to see what rig modifications others may have and how difficult the trail is in your opinion. You can also ask someone with experience on that trail, but their opinion may vary considerably from another person's opinion or your own.

Sand Driving

Driving in sand is a unique experience. Sand comes in many varieties and can change with moisture content. It is very easy to lose traction in sand. At low speeds, adding power will induce wheelspin. The tires will quickly dig into the sand in most conditions. It is not unusual to see a vehicle buried up to the frame or door sills in sand. Being stuck in sand can be very difficult.

Dry sand ranges from larger particles to a very fine silt almost with the consistency of talcum powder. More coarse sand will support weight better than fine sand. In all cases, some speed is needed to maintain momentum and break through the sand. Some speed is necessary even on flat sections. More speed is needed on climbs, and momentum is still necessary when blasting down sand dunes.

If the sand is damp (as opposed to wet), it is easier to drive on. Wet sand supports more weight and less speed is needed to keep from being sucked into the surface.

Wheelspin acts like a paddle wheel helping drive the vehicle forward. Significant wheelspin is good in the sand, especially when climbing and even descending sand dunes.

Little power is needed to induce wheelspin in sand. Carrying speed is always important, so running in four-wheel-drive high range is preferable to low range, especially if the climb is long and steep.

Steering input should be gentle. Sharp and/or abrupt steering inputs can cause the front tires to continue in a straight line, rather than steer on the desired path. When this occurs, it's like putting on the brakes. Getting stuck is very possible. So, go easy with steering inputs.

Large, Steep Sand Dunes

Large sand dunes are generally composed of soft, fine sand blown by wind into rounded slopes at the top on the windward side, while the back (leeward) side has steep slopes near the top. Climbing the back side requires considerable speed to make it over the crest. Most often, the slope of the sand dune on the back side will become considerably steeper as the crest is approached. Carrying speed is paramount. Fine-grain sand can slow the vehicle very quickly unless momentum is maintained. Power should be applied until the rear tires clear the crest.

When climbing the wind-blown side, power should be applied until the crest is reached. At the top, be aware of a steep drop off. Turning along the ridge is one option, but steering must be precise. Reducing speed as the crest is reached improves control. After the steepest part of the descent, power can be applied to maintain momentum.

Since large sand dunes require both speed and traction, use four-wheel-drive high range. Tire pressures should be reduced to the lowest practical pressure (10 to 12 psi for a non-beadlock wheel and even lower with beadlock wheels). If your rig is equipped with lockers that function in four-wheel-drive high range, use the lockers. If steering is ineffective with the front locker engaged, disengage it. Large sand dunes require caution when approaching the top of the dune. If approaching from the backside, momentum needs to be carried over the lip of the dune. When approaching from the wind-direction side, speed needs to be reduced as the top is crested to avoid the steep drop-off and possibly becoming airborne.

Outdoor and off-road enthusiasts across America now have access to Ford's Bronco Off-Roadeo through the newly designed Half-Day Adventure at one of four unique US locations.

The Half-Day Adventure at Bronco Off-Roadeo is a four-hour, paid, off-road quest with trail-guide instruction. Participants of all skill levels are welcome, and a Bronco will be provided for use throughout the experience. The Half-Day Adventure is an abbreviated version of the classic 10-hour day, which is offered as a complimentary benefit exclusively to new Bronco, Bronco Raptor, and Bronco Sport owners.

The Bronco's off-roading capabilities are made possible with its exclusive Terrain Management System with G.O.A.T. modes (designed to help drivers better navigate any type of terrain) and off-road mapping and drive technologies, such as the Bronco Trail app and Trail Control.

Source Guide

Bestop
333 Centennial Pkwy. Suite B
Louisville, CO 80027
800-845-3567
bestop.com

Bronc Buster
726-225-2134
broncbustertx.com

Bronco Nation Store
gear.thebronconation.com

Bronco Off-Roadeo
broncooffroadeo.com

CJ Pony Parts
7461 Allentown Blvd.
Harrisburg, PA 17112
800-888-6473
cjponyparts.com/
   ford-bronco-parts/c/4096/

Ecklers Parts & Accessories
877-305-8966
ecklers.com

Everything Bronco Aftermarket
2544 American Dr.
Appleton, WI 54914
(920) 570-6684
everythingbroncoaftermarket
   .com

Extreme Terrain Offroad
   Outfitters
877-870-8556
extremeterrain.com

Ford Parts
fordparts.com
844-589-0060

Forged 4x4
4867 Mercury St.
San Diego, CA 92111
530-680-0426
forged4x4.com

Four Wheel Parts
877-474-4821
4wheelparts.com

Foutz Motorsports LLC
4725 E. Ivy St. #102
Mesa, AZ 85205
480-718-9800
foutzmotorsports.com

IAG Off-Road
1241 New Windsor Rd.
Westminster, MD 21158
410-840-3555
iagoffroad.com

Jeff's Bronco Graveyard
7843 Lochlin Dr.
Brighton, MI 48116
248-437-5060
broncograveyard.com

NexGen Bronco Parts &
   Accessories
51532 Finch Ln.
Independence, LA 70443
888-635-7895
nexgenbronco.com

Northridge 4x4
7976 Rubicon Trail Pl. NW
Silverdale, WA 98383
360-340-0282
northridge4x4.com

Rock Slide Engineering
2587 N. 200 W.
North Logan, UT 84341
435-752-4580
rockslideengineering.com

74Weld Motorsports
9349 Bond Ave.
El Cajon, CA 92021
619-286-6656
motorsports.74weld.com

Shock Surplus
12711 Ramona Blvd. #106
Irwindale, CA 91706
213-433-3616
shocksurplus.com

Summit Racing
1-800-230-3030
summitracing.com

Toms Offroad
2065 Lars Way
Medford, OR 97501
541-779-1339
tomsoffroad.com

Wild Horses 4x4
1045 S. Cherokee Ln.
Lodi, CA 95240
209-400-7200
wildhorses4x4.com

Wilwood Disc Brakes
805-388-1188
wilwood.com